D1540874

Advanced Studies in Handwriting Psychology

Seven Original Monographs

by Sheila R. Lowe, MS, CG, CFDE

Also by Sheila Lowe

Advanced Studies in Handwriting Psychology
Personality & Anxiety Disorders
Sheila Lowe's Handwriting Analyzer software
www.sheilalowe.com

The Forensic Handwriting Mysteries

POISON PEN
WRITTEN IN BLOOD
DEAD WRITE
LAST WRITES
INKSLINGERS BALL
OUTSIDE The LINES
WRITTEN OFF

WHAT SHE SAW
PROOF OF LIFE

Audiobooks:
What She Saw
Written Off
Inkslingers Ball

www.claudiaroseseries.com

Table of Contents

Introduction

The monographs included in this volume are the result of a study and practice in the field of handwriting analysis that began in 1967 and continues through today. Sheila Lowe holds a Master's degree in psychology and is a court-qualified forensic handwriting expert who has taught in the extension programs at UC Riverside and UC Santa Barbara (her curriculum vitae is included in an appendix). She has served as president of the American Handwriting Analysis Foundation since 2011. The author of handwriting analysis software and several books, as well as monographs and articles concerning the topic of handwriting analysis, Sheila also writes a mystery series featuring fictional handwriting expert Claudia Rose.

The material presented in this book is with the expectation that the reader is familiar with the basic principles of gestalt graphology (handwriting analysis). For those who wish to pursue a serious study in this field, Sheila's Self-Study Program in Gestalt Graphology is available through her website. Sheila makes herself available to provide feedback and help to all of her students. A certificate of completion is awarded upon demonstration of a clear understanding of the material by correctly answering a series of questions. Even those who have studied the trait-stroke method taught by IGAS find they benefit from rounding out their knowledge with the gestalt method.

What is the difference between the two methods? Trait-stroke is an empirical method that views handwriting stroke-by-stroke. This provides a small field of vision as if looking through a microscope, where the analyst makes a laundry list of traits piece-by-piece and builds them into a personality profile. The trait-stroke method assigns a personality trait name to each stroke of writing, such as "resentment strokes," or "yieldingness strokes."

The gestalt method comes from the holistic end of the spectrum. Gestalt analysts view handwriting as three pictures: spatial arrangement, writing form (letter design), and writing movement. It is akin to looking through a telescope and seeing the handwriting as a whole picture. The basic principle of the gestalt method is that no single stroke is significant outside the context of the handwriting under analysis.

While the logical, step-by-step thinker tends to be more attracted to the trait-stroke method, and the more conceptual, "big picture" thinker prefers the gestalt method, a well-trained analyst should reach similar conclusions regardless of which they use.

Happy analyzing!

Signs of Childhood Sexual Abuse
Seen in the Handwriting of Adults

Signs of Childhood Sexual Abuse Seen in the Handwriting of Adults

© Sheila Lowe 2006

All rights reserved. No part of this monograph may be reproduced in any form without express permission by the author.

www.sheilalowe.com www.superceu.com

Signs of childhood sexual abuse seen in the handwriting of adults

At the close of a handwriting analysis conference, six women met in a coffee shop to discuss the program they had just attended on sexual abuse. As the conversation went around the table, five of the six indicated that they had themselves been sexually abused in childhood to one degree or another. The sixth joked that she felt left out, having been raised in a "normal nuclear family" where everyone was treated with respect.

Childhood sexual abuse, of course, is no joke. Some research indicates that 27% percent of women and at least 10% of men have reported experiencing childhood sexual trauma. Other studies claim that the figures may actually be much higher–more than fifty percent of women–as this crime often goes unreported.

Because many victims grow up burdened by profound feelings of shame, as if they were the perpetrator rather than the victim, they keep the abuse secret, never revealing what happened to them. This is especially true of male victims who were raised with the belief that men must always be strong, self-confident, always in control. Consequently, being victimized in this way makes a boy or young man feel that he is weak, less than a man, which makes him even more reluctant than a female victim to admit what happened to him.

As a projective behavior, the handwriting of a victim who has not dealt with his or her sexual abuse is likely to include signs of the unresolved issues. By identifying some of these signs, possibly even before the client raises the issue, the handwriting professional will have an additional tool to help him or her gain insight that can be helpful to the client and/or therapist.

Of course, handwriting cannot reveal specifics about the abuse, such as exactly what happened or who the perpetrators were, or the exact ages at which it took place, but it can identify some of the defenses and coping mechanisms employed by the victim, which may not be working to his or her benefit.

We will be examining some case histories along with handwriting samples to illustrate the global and some specific characteristics that point to unresolved childhood sexual abuse in adult men and women.

Who are the abusers?

To be considered an abuser, the perpetrator must be older than the victim. Some state laws say that s/he must be at least five years older, and some require, depending upon the age of the victim, that there be more than 2-3 years difference in age between abuser and victim.

In most cases, the abuser is known to the child but is not a relative. In 60% of reported cases, a family friend, neighbor, or babysitter is responsible. About half that number–30%–

the child's father, grandfather, brother, cousin, or uncle. The remaining 10% include stranger abductions or another perpetrator unknown to the child. Boys, more than girls, are likely to be abused by strangers or authority figures such as coaches, religious leaders, or teachers.

Sexual abuse is not limited to male perpetrators. Although the numbers are far lower in cases of female abusers, it is estimated that women are the abuser in at least 14% of cases against male victims and 6% against females. The family in which rampant drug and/or alcohol abuse is found provides an especially fertile ground for sexual abuse.

Children who are experiencing or who have experienced sexual abuse exhibit a variety of behaviors including nightmares, inappropriate sexual behavior or seductiveness, play that acts out the abuse, and sudden bedwetting after toilet training. Boys tend to act out, sometimes treating smaller children or animals badly, or running away. Some children become depressed and withdrawn. Some will harm themselves or even attempt suicide. If these behaviors are not properly addressed early on, the stage is set for serious problems that continue into adulthood and may impact the person's whole life.

What constitutes sexual abuse?

What types of behaviors constitute sexual abuse? They run the gamut from inappropriate kissing, touching and fondling, to various types of intercourse–anal, oral, vaginal. "Inappropriate" is a key word in determining whether a behavior should be labeled abuse. There is a world of difference between a loving grandfather planting an affectionate kiss on a five-year-old's cheek and one who forces a French kiss on her or slips a hand down her panties. Even a small child instinctively knows the difference.

If a little girl is unable or unwilling to seek help for issues of sexual abuse, she is liable to suffer from anxiety or depression and will find it difficult to trust in relationships as she grows into a young woman and then an adult. Women who have not received help dealing with past abuse often place themselves in situations that recreate the abuse. Despite that it perpetuates feelings of shame and guilt, such situations feel familiar. These tendencies appear in their handwriting.

Not only is there a higher incidence of drug and alcohol abuse in sexual abuse victims of both genders, numerous physiological conditions are also more prevalent than in the general population. In women, diabetes, asthma, chronic pelvic pain, headache, eating disorders, gastrointestinal problems and a host of other ailments are seen. Obesity is common, with the extra weight these women carry serving as a deterrent against further abuse by literally creating a barrier between the woman and a potential abuser. Eating disorders are especially common if the sexual assault included oral sex that resulted in ejaculation in the victim's mouth.

In addition to physiological ailments, psychological problems arise, which may include post-traumatic stress, anxiety, withdrawal, poor self-esteem, self-mutilation, poor body image, sexual problems, suicidal ideation and/or actual attempts. Due to widely fluctuating attitudes in relationships, and the repetitive self-harming behaviors in which these clients so often engage, borderline personality disorder is a frequent diagnosis. Many of these symptoms also appear in handwriting.

Dissociative disorders may be present. According to Erica Sharkansky, Ph.D., "Dissociation can involve a range of phenomena from altered awareness or attention to flashbacks and out of body experiences. Dissociation is usually triggered by a strong emotional reaction such as feelings of terror, surprise, shame, or helplessness, or such as feeling trapped or exposed." Even in a non-threatening environment, such as a doctor's office, being asked to remove clothing or being touched can spark a reaction far beyond what might be expected under those circumstances.

The victim's attitude toward sex may become polarized, either avoiding sexual situations altogether, being unable to respond sexually, or finding sexual contact physically painful. At the other end of the spectrum, they may be hypersexual or promiscuous.

Research conducted at the California School of Professional Psychology at Fresno, California suggests that a significantly higher percentage of lesbian women—22%—experienced childhood molestation than heterosexual women. This was compared to 1% of heterosexual women and 7% of heterosexual men. It is reported that many lesbian women appear to have been abused by male relatives.

Male Victims

When both abuser and victim are male, the young victim is more likely to grow up questioning his sexual identity or sexual preference than female victims do when abused by a female. Interesting to note, when the abuser is a female, the male may not be seen by society as a victim. There have been some high-profile cases, however, like that of Mary Kay LaTourneau, a 34-year-old teacher who admitted to having a sexual relationship with her thirteen-year-old student and then bearing his children, where a prison sentence resulted. A discussion specific to abusers, though, is a subject for another monograph.

Men victimized in childhood or as teenagers generally have some different emotional and physiological symptoms than women. Fearing that they may "become gay," some men try to prove their masculinity by having many female partners or adopting "macho" behaviors. Clinical Social Worker Peter Dimmock of the Male Survivor organization says, "Males are more likely to act out the sexual abuse aggressively, and report more frequently than females a desire to hurt others." Yet, despite a widely held belief that victims generally grow up to be abusers, recent research disputes this belief as myth.

Additionally, in an article in the British Journal of Psychiatry we learn that, although a victim-abuser cycle exists in a minority of male perpetrators, the same is not true for female victims. Other articles reviewed tended to support this view. In a study conducted by Campbell, Glasser, Leitch, and Farrelly, a total of 843 subjects were interviewed, of which 747 were male and 96 were female. Of the male subjects, 35% of perpetrators had been victims of childhood sexual abuse and 11% of non-perpetrators. Of 96 female subjects, 43% had been victims, but only one became a perpetrator. Thus, of the total number of subjects, 73% were not abusers.

The BJP article notes that background factors tended to include alcohol abuse, violence, unemployment, absence of adults at home, marital problems, and sexual problems (deviation or dysfunction). Because these factors are likely to influence the quality of parenting, they can be expected to affect the way a child views parent figures and other relationships. Their conclusion: "Bolton et al (1989) suggests that it is only a minority of males who do so [repeat the abuse in the next generation]. There is also little or no evidence of a cycle in the general population (or in females)."

The finer details of the victim-abuser demographic makeup are beyond the scope of this monograph, whose main goal is to describe the syndrome of personality traits generally seen in adults who were sexually abused as children and correlate some of those traits with handwriting characteristics.

While women tend to turn their feelings inward, resulting in depression, as noted above, men are more likely to act out, sometimes violently, sometimes through promiscuous and/or unsafe sex. In addition to post traumatic stress, depression and other anxiety disorders, substance abuse occurs in 80% of male victims, compared to 11% of men who were not abused. Many of the physiological symptoms that women experience also occur in men, with the addition of encopresis (bowel incontinence).

An article by Richard J. Corelli, M.D., suggests that women who are victims of incest during childhood have a much greater incidence of borderline personality disorder. He states, "This chronic or periodic victimization and sometimes brutalization can later result in impaired relationships and mistrust of men and excessive preoccupation with sexuality, sexual promiscuity, inhibitions, deep-seated depression and a seriously damaged self-image."

As you will see below, several of the handwriting samples to be discussed would qualify for borderline personality disorder in terms of the behaviors that are symptomatic of that disorder.

Some handwriting characteristics common to sexual abuse victims

Let's review some of the behaviors exhibited by both adult men and women who have experienced sexual abuse in childhood, but who have not received adequate help or support:

> ➢ *Depression*
> ➢ *Anxiety*
> ➢ *Poor self-esteem*
> ➢ *Sexual problems*
> ➢ *Dissociation*
> ➢ *Potential for violent acting out*
> ➢ *Overcontrolling in relationships*

Although this monograph points to some specific areas in which signs of sexual abuse may be seen, it is important to understand that every handwriting sample must be viewed as a whole entity of which those areas are a part. No single element, such as the way a t is crossed or an i dotted, has any meaning by itself.

In other words, the "meaning" of a particular handwriting characteristic can change, depending upon other characteristics that surround it (context). Look at the writing as if it were a picture. This concept will become clearer as we examine some examples in a moment. First, though, we introduce some of the general handwriting characteristics related to each of the behaviors above, with the understanding that because handwriting is unique to each writer, there are many more possibilities than can be covered in this article.

Depression: a condition of general emotional dejection and withdrawal

The depressed person feels sad, lacks energy for and interest in the activities of everyday life. Think of the such a person's body language. The head is down, shoulders droop. You can tell it's an effort just to put one foot in front of the other.

Handwriting is much like body language. In the depressed person's handwriting, there is a slackness in the rhythm as the writing moves from left-to-right across the page. The writing looks lifeless and may actually droop in places. The baseline points downward, a sign of fatigue, discouragement, or illness. This writer has all but given up on life. He feels as if trying to improve things is wasted effort.

Interestingly, a baseline with an extreme uphill slant may also point to a writer who is depressed. The difference is, the uphill writer keeps working at maintaining a positive mental outlook and tries to pull himself up out of his despondency. There are times, too, when someone who has made the decision to take his own life feels such a sense of relief that his handwriting becomes buoyant. As always, handwriting reveals emotion and behavior at the moment it is written. It is not a predictor of future events.

5

Anxiety: an overwhelming feeling of discomfort, tension, or uneasiness

Anxiety has been called an indefinable fear of something in the future. In the anxious person, the fight or flight mechanism is always engaged, which place the muscles in a constant state of tension. Unpleasant repetitive thoughts plague him most of the time.

The handwriting of the chronically anxious person may have a jumpy, nervous appearance. The overall rhythm has an irregular staccato appearance, like a tap dancer who is dancing as fast as he can. This type of writing tends to be simplified, with extra loops and strokes cut off. This stripped-down appearance represents the person who is always on the alert and ready for action (fight or flight). He doesn't add anything elaborate to the writing because he feels strung out, unable to take on anything more (Anxiety is covered in greater depth in another paper by the same author, which addresses personality disorders.)

Poor self-esteem: a lack of confidence, mistrust of self and others

The person with poor self-esteem feels stupid, unattractive, can do nothing right. Any obstacle is too large to attempt overcoming. Feeling as if she has nothing to offer, she finds it difficult to make friends. When she receives a compliment, she finds it hard to accept or refuses to believe it. Even very attractive and intelligent young women who have been abused may believe that something is wrong with them, that they don't deserve love or happiness. Their belligerent, chip-on-the-shoulder attitude holds others at bay. Although some people with poor self-esteem may be able to mask it with a cheerful, happy-go-lucky exterior, inside they are suffering.

The handwriting of someone with healthy self-esteem has a generally balanced appearance, with good proportions and organization. The margins will be more or less even, the spaces between the words is neither too wide nor too narrow. The form of the writing will be natural and pleasant. There won't be a sense that something is wrong with it.

The writing (most often female writers) of someone with poor self-esteem often has extremely rounded, large writing with short capital letters. Or, at the opposite end of the spectrum, the handwriting may be very small, as if it was shrinking right off the page.

Capital letters, especially the personal pronoun I (PPI), reveal a great deal about the person's self-esteem, and represent the ideal self. The lowercase letters such as "o," "a," "s," "m," "n," symbolize the real self.

A disproportionally large discrepancy in height between the capitals and lowercase indicates a possible problem with reality testing. To make a determination, according to US copybooks, the formula for proportion between capital/lowercase is for the capital letters to be approximately 2-2 ½ times the height of lower case letters. Anything taller than three times the height suggests an out-of-control ego.

With the exception of Russian Cyrillic, English is the only language where a single letter, the personal pronoun "I," (PPI) is used to represent the writer. This makes it a very important letter. If this letter is exaggerated or stands out in any way, such as looking bloated, having sharp angles, or is very rounded and looks like a fetus, this is a good indicator for poor self-esteem.

Sexual problems: difficulty with desire, arousal, or resolution of sexual activity

A lack of desire for sexual contact, or inability to become aroused even when with a loving, considerate partner, is often a carryover from unresolved sexual trauma. Or, paraphilias—sexual activities that lie outside the norm—commonly described as "kinky sex," may be a way of acting out sexual issues. For this paper, the specific sexual activities in which a person may choose to engage are not important. What is important are the indications in handwriting that the writer obtains sexual gratification in ways that are generally considered outside the norm. Of course, there is some subjectivity in how that is defined!

Although it is vital that one firmly remember that all parts of handwriting reveal information about the way the writer thinks, feels, and behaves, for our purposes, it is useful to explore some specific handwriting elements. The lower loops seem particularly to reflect sexual attitudes and issues.

First, note that the baseline, which is the invisible or printed line on which we write, is the dividing line between the conscious and the unconscious. Any writing that sits on the line or rises above it is in the area of the conscious and the writer's day-to-day activities. Anything that dips below the line is in the area of the unconscious, which specifically represents the writer's past and sexual urges (among other things).

So, after drawing the circle on the "g" or the "bucket" on the y, both of which are above the baseline, standard US copybooks require the writer to form a downstroke that is intended to plunge below the baseline, turn and make a curve at the bottom, then travel back up to completion at the baseline.

In making these movements, the writer is symbolically going down into the subconscious, which includes past memories and experiences. The late great graphologist Felix Klein compared it to dipping a bucket into a well. When the bucket is full, you bring it back up and use the contents. In handwriting, the pen goes into the well of the lower zone and brings back up lessons learned from the past to use in daily life.

But what if the downstroke is left hanging in the lower zone with no return stroke? Or what if the return stroke turns in a direction other than straight back to the baseline, or makes extra loops, ties, or little tics? Such formations are almost invariably rooted in unresolved sexual issues.

Dissociation: splitting off a group of mental processes from the main body of consciousness

Repeated sexual abuse in childhood, especially in cases where the mother was perceived by the child as unavailable, is one cause of adult dissociation. Research by Barbara Apgar, MD indicates that early separation from a parent was related to sexual and physical abuse, and because dysfunctional behaviors were reported in mothers more often than fathers, attachment problems are at least in part related to dissociation. "Patients who reported having mothers who drank heavily experienced the most significant dissociative symptoms," says Apgar.

Dissociation may be seen to some degree in handwriting where lowercase letters above the baseline (in the middle zone) break down and become formless, making words illegible. These disintegrating letters represent the ego in distress. Extra-wide spaces between words add to a sense of isolation and unreality. These large spaces make islands out of individual words and form a pattern that looks like a river as they progress down the page. Assuming no visual problems that affect handwriting, when "rivers" are present, they symbolize an inner emotional split.

The copybook standard for word spacing is that the distance between words should be approximately the width of a letter "m" in that particular handwriting. If most words are closer than that, they are too close. If they are much further apart, they are too far.

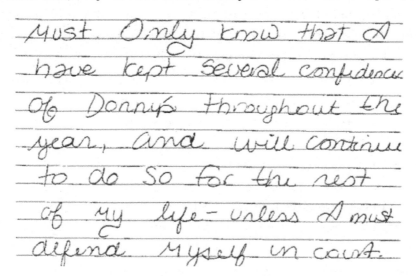

The above sample is a schoolteacher who was acquitted of charges that she bribed a 15-year-old student with gifts and other benefits in exchange for sex, and other charges that included sexual relations with a minor but was convicted of contributing to the delinquency of a minor.

While the teacher's personal background is unknown to this author, in the handwriting, we see the rivers of space between that sometimes appear in people who themselves were abused and who dissociate or detach themselves from the feelings.

Potential for violent acting out: Impulsive and uncontrollable outbursts

It has been observed in several studies that women in treatment express sadness about the abuse at the beginning of treatment, and only begin to experience their anger toward the end. Men, on the other hand, begin with anger and express their sadness only later.

Anger and antisocial characteristics in handwriting appear in extremely heavy, and sometimes extremely light, pressure on the paper. Those who adopt extremely heavy pen pressure are symbolically acting out against the environment. They perseverate, grinding the pen into the paper so that "i" dots, periods or other punctuation stand out from the handwriting as heavy black dots.

When *heavy* pressure combines with a strong rightward slant on upper loops such as "l," "b," "h," the writer's behavior tends to be angry and impulsive, likely to be acted out against others. The following sample is a good example.

On the other hand, extremely *light* pressure represents one who is every bit as angry as the heavy-pressured writer, but who turns the anger inward on himself. The writing is so light that it barely touches the paper, as if the writer cannot bear to feel anything and pushes negative feelings away. Of course, those feelings have to go somewhere.

Like a pressure cooker, over time, frustration and anger builds to a boiling point. Absent an outlet, when an eruption finally occurs, the damage to self and others can be severe and long-lasting, even to the point of homicide and suicide, which is the case with the writer of the next sample.

Note: pressure is not necessarily determined by physical strength. The writer, a 34-year-old left-handed male, 6'4, was a federal agent and no shrinking violet. The pressure in his sample is extremely light.

Overcontrolling in relationships: Dominating a partner

Some adult victims, in their attempt to feel that they are finally in charge of their own lives, feel the need to control everything and everyone around them. Rather than developing a loving relationship where feelings and experiences are shared, they create rules for their partner and insist on being The Boss in the relationship.

The person who needs to control others is demonstrating an exaggerated external reaction to the internal fear that the abuse may happen again if he fails to keep everything in his environment under his thumb.

Often, the controlling person's handwriting tends to be rigid, with a linear appearance, rather than a balance of curves and straight lines. There may be hooks on the beginnings of endings of words. Upper loops are likely to be retraced, which suggests closed-mindedness and rigidity of thought and action. Disproportionately tall upper loops, display an authoritarian personality. The spatial arrangement of the controlling person's writing tends to be crowded, with letters, words, and lines crammed too close together. The following sample contains a phenomenon known as the "domineering t-bar."

order form is a r g

My life has been hard by my standards
and according to friends, I was born under
a shinning star - When things were at
their lowest point and my back against
the wall, out of nowhere something good
linstens to me and always for the best —

Secrecy and Denial

An abuser often threatens harm to the child and/or their family members if they tell what happened to them. Thus, secrecy and denial are strongly associated with childhood sexual abuse.

The oval letters, "o" and "a" (because these letters are the easiest to check) should be

Doug tells me that you are one of the top handwriting analysts in the country.

I would really appreciate it if you could analyze my handwriting to reveal my personality.

clear and free from extra loops or hooks, which interfere with clear communication. Letters that are completely encircled before they move to the right suggest denial and difficulty in communicating in a direct manner. In fact, that particular form is most often seen in the handwritings of adults who were raised in a family where everyone was expected to keep the family secrets of alcoholism or sexual abuse.

Part Two – Case histories

Important note: As we move into exploring actual handwriting samples, it must be emphasized again that what is described are some of the more obvious characteristics that point to unresolved sexual abuse issues. The competent handwriting professional will always look at the whole picture in which these obvious characteristics fit. Of course, not all characteristics will be present in every handwriting.

Something else to remember: because a client's handwriting has a good gestalt and appears more or less healthy does not necessarily mean that there was no abuse in his or her background. If someone has done the necessary work in therapy or has received some other type of help to resolve some of the issues caused by those painful experiences and grow past the abuse, over time, the person's handwriting will change to reflect changes in their behavior. It can often be illuminating to ask that client to write about sexual activity or anything connected with sex. As in the next sample, marked signs of anxiety may suddenly appear.

This sample has many obvious problems that go beyond the scope of this specific discussion. It is being used here to demonstrate how handwriting can change depending on the content being written about.

The sample is part of a statement given to police by a young woman who filed a report of sexual assault against several individuals. As you can see, her handwriting begins to change as she gets into her story and she becomes agitated. Whether or not she is being entirely truthful about the alleged assault is another matter. The emotionally charged material becomes more right-slanted and urgent.

Amber, 52

When Amber was a toddler her father died and her mother remarried. She was three years old when her stepfather began to sexually abuse her. Her mother divorced this man, but the next boyfriend took up the abuse, and the next. Eventually, there was a total of five perpetrators, who included Amber's older sister's husband, and a landlord who threatened to kill Amber and her entire family if she revealed what he had done. It was not until she was twelve that the sexual abuse finally ended.

Amber claims to hate her verbally and mentally abusive mother, who, after learning of one of the instances of sexual abuse, called her a whore and told her she would never amount to anything. Perhaps predictably, Amber became pregnant at 17. She married the baby's father, but subsequently divorced him, then remarried. This time the marriage lasted only a few weeks when she came to understand that her new husband was unwilling to accept the responsibility of a wife and child.

> Kody, I really wanted you. We didn't know what sex he was until he was born. And the doctor cried out "its a girl" So I went running down the hall yelling "its a girl, its a girl!" Then as I got to the double Doors he called out "No, its a boy." Well it turned out good anyway because we bonded two weeks before he was born. There was a spiritual bond there.

Amber and her current husband have been married for more than twenty years and operate their own business. She enjoys wearing a lot of jewelry and paints her fingernails in bright glittery colors. Acquaintances describe her as having a childlike manner and "very likable and sweet."

At about 100 pounds overweight, she is diabetic and suffers from congestive heart failure. Amber is also under the care of a psychiatrist who has for many years prescribed anti-depressants for her.

Amber's handwriting is overly rounded and has a childlike appearance. She has an emotional age or around twelve. Her emotional growth clock stopped at approximately the same age as did the sexual abuse.

The roundedness demonstrates her likeable, sweet nature and is reminiscent of a friendly puppy. Although pressure can only be reliably determined by viewing the original sample, Amber writes with heavy pressure, an indicator of her unresolved anger.

Sweetness notwithstanding, anger is present, too, in the stunted lower zone. The loops are proportionally far too short for the writing size. Also, they turn to the left, toward mother, seeking nurturing. They are retraced, as in the word "good" in the third line from the bottom, which demonstrates a fear of opening up sexually. The baseline moves uphill for a few lines, indicating her desire to be optimistic and cheery (note: she's writing about a subject that makes her happy).

By the fourth line, the baseline sags downheartedly. The baseline and words begin to fluctuate, with some words pointing upward and some downward; the slant of the upper loops shifts from one direction to another. This suggests that it's hard for Amber to set a goal and stick with it as she has to cope with many changing emotions.

In any handwriting, the first stroke of the pen in each single letter or word symbolizes mother and the final stroke symbolizes father. Although most modern copybooks teach the student to make the top loop of the PPI first, Amber's Capital I begins at the bottom with a cramped hooked stroke, which indicates her negative feelings toward her mother. The top part, where she ends the letter, has a nice loop, idealizing her deceased father.

Note, on the second line, the two lower parts of the y's actually form an arc rather than a loop. This is a symbolic covering over of the sexual abuse she experienced in the past (below the baseline).

For reasons of privacy, her signature is not included. However, suffice it to say, she signs her name far away from the text, which represents a lack of integration between how she sees herself and the self she presents to the world.

"No Name," 41

The next sample was written by a professional woman with a reported history of unresolved sexual abuse. She is alcohol-dependent (she describes it as "binge drinking"), and her behavior is emotionally unstable, impulsive, and volatile. After having had no committed relationship with a man for six years while raising her young son she subsequently entered two relationships that she termed "catch and release."

Supposedly ready to be exclusive in a relationship, "No name" asked a man for an immediate commitment on a first date. Following an evening of drinking, she expressed concern that time was running out for her and said she needed to move quickly. She fell apart emotionally, demanding clarification of the man's intentions and plans and whether he had been seeing other women.

Hello, my name is no name.
born and raised in Wisconsin
sitting next to N.Y.
fourth week at the group.
going to keep it up.
nothing more to say.
bye.

"No Name's" handwriting is simplified, with few extra strokes or loops, which indicates the ability to get quickly to the heart of a matter. While there is intelligence present, the writing is carelessly written with low regularity in the letter designs, which vacillates from cursive to printing and back, showing inconsistency and unevenness of temperament and behavior.

The extremely wide spaces left between the words are an indicator of isolation, of feeling alone in her pain, unable to socialize with others in appropriate ways. The overall writing is soft and a flabby-looking, lacking the rhythm that would give it strength.

Mixed with the slack movement, the baseline attempts a pronounced uphill slant. It's as if No Name feels like the mythical Sisyphus, condemned for all eternity to push a rock up a hill, only to have it slide back down every time he reached the top.

Sisyphus' penalty for offending the gods was, in effect, that he must perform futile and hopeless labor, the worst punishment of all. No Name does her best to keep her chin up, and even while she fears all is hopeless, keeps pushing forward, just in case her luck turns.

As is so frequently true of abuse victims, the lower "loops" are not loops at all, but merely pitiful little sticks. In some cases, such as the "y" in the first line, they are cut off with an angry little tic at the bottom. When she dips her symbolic bucket into the well of the past, she's afraid of what she might draw up, so she leaves the bucket down there and refuses to look at the painful material.

The "g" in the third line is malformed, which might be a result of intoxication (handwriting changes under the influence). In any case, there is a problem in forming the lower loops, which is the area that encompasses sexual values, desires, and attitudes.

Finally, in the third line and the fifth, she has over-written some letters. Again, intoxication may play a part, or it's possible there could be a neurological issue, such as petit mal seizures. It could also be due to anxiety caused by a compulsion to go back and correct things that don't look as good as she would like them to, trying to make them look better.

Clarke, 35

This man suffered unspecified childhood sexual abuse and is in treatment for violent behavior.

Clarke's handwriting is linear and is lacking sufficient curves for yin/yang balance. The writing is simplified and shows intelligence, but the rigid strokes give it an angry, resentful appearance. The first thing that draws the eye are the dark spots created by overwriting. This is a sign of perseveration and unreleased tension. Black spots in handwriting can be symbolic of an actual "black spot" in the writer's past, of which he is ashamed and is trying to cover up. The too-wide spaces between words reveal Clark's isolation from others. He writes at a downhill slant, which is often a sign of depression or negative thinking. The linear forms create poor rhythm, which indicates that he has difficulty releasing his strong feelings. Thus, the feelings build up and eventually find an outlet, when he will act out, sometimes violently.

The heavy downstrokes, such as on the stem of the letter "t" are a sign of dogmatism and insistence on having things his own way. Some of the upper loops are disproportionately tall, which reveal an authoritarian personality.

#1

The extreme right slant of the writing, most easily seen in upper loops, indicates poor impulse control and a proneness to aggressive outbursts. It would be no surprise if he was given a diagnosis of intermittent explosive disorder.

Jay, 25

Jay's handwriting is undeveloped, childlike in appearance. It shows average intellectual capacity but below average emotional maturity. His handwriting suggests an emotional age of around fourteen.

The writing is printed, which symbolically cuts off the ligatures (connections) between letters. Ligatures represent social connections. When removed, the writer may be friendly and outgoing, but has difficulty forming and maintaining truly intimate bonds.

... compared with a woman, a man _____

18. When I make a mistake _I try to fix it_

19. When I was a child, I didn't like _getting beatin + molested_

20. I am _a very good person, People don't think so_

21. A good friend _will always be there for you_

22. Something important about my father _I like was He showed me everything I kn_

23. When I was young my problem was _Nobody understood me_

24. For me a commitment is _for life_

25. I can lose control _Sometimes but not to the Point of violence_

The word spacing is too close. Jay had limited space in which to write, but on some lines where he could have used more room he chose not to, so we can assume that this close spacing is his natural mode, suggesting a need for closeness. As discussed above, squeezing the letters and words together is contrary to the social distance of printed forms. This

17

indicates an inner conflict: he needs social contact but is afraid to reveal himself on anything more than a superficial level.

The writing slant fluctuates widely, which reveals labile emotions. As in the previous samples, the lower "loops" are unfinished. In Jay's case they sometimes form a cradle, such as the "g" on the line beginning with #20. The stroke moves to the left, which seeks mothering and nurturing that he evidently felt was missing in his early life. In several places, the downstroke of the "y" is short and weak–he is afraid to look too far into the past. At the same time, he states on line #19 that he didn't like getting beaten and molested as a child (who would!). Thus, he is able to talk about and intellectualize what happened to him, but he doesn't deal with it on an emotional level.

In several places, the letter "d" is formed like a hook ("felon's claw"). Hooks hold on to things or feelings. Jay has been unable to let go of his painful past experiences because he can't look at them (the stunted lower "loops").

In his signature, which is not included for reasons of privacy, he protectively loops the initial of his last name around the first name, then ends that initial with a slashing stroke which effectively goes through the last name (though the slash is made first), representative of a hostile act, possibly toward his father, who gave him the name.

Brenda, 40

At 7 years old Brenda was molested by an uncle over a period of several months. When she reported the abuse to her parents her father became angry and refused to believe her, stating that his brother would never do such a thing. She grew up abusing drugs and alcohol on and off for a long period of time, but was finally able to get clean and sober through A.A.

Much later, as an adult, with her mother secretly listening in, Brenda confronted her uncle on a phone call, asking him whether her memory of the sexual abuse was accurate. He admitted it, broke down and cried, begged for her forgiveness, which she was willing to give. When she told her father of his brother's confession, he responded that it was all in the past and they should forget it.

Brenda's handwriting has a slightly emphasis on rounded forms but is more balanced than the ones we have examined so far. Notwithstanding all the work she has done in therapy, and that she is a longtime member of AA, signs of her history remain in her handwriting.

Remember: handwriting changes over time as the writer grows and undergoes many life experiences. Someone who is able to successfully work through their early sexual abuse issues can expect to see eventual changes in their handwriting.

> I have spend many years in therapy and a in recovery working on these issues. I feel I'm one of the fortunate ones who was able to realize that my only part in it was continuing to be the victim in my adult life. Once I took control of my own destiny and took responsibility for my own actions, I was able to forgive my Uncle and my Dad. It was in the forgiving that God set me free.

The loops of Brenda's personal pronoun I (PPI) are separated at top and bottom, which is often seen in the handwriting of one whose parents did not see eye to eye. It may be that the parents were separated physically, ideologically, or both. Note, too, the PPI is rounded and tends to fall over to the right. The right is historically symbolic of father and authority figures. This "falling over" suggests that despite her disappointment in her father, Brenda accepts him for who he is.

The long, curved initial strokes reveal that Brenda holds on to what has served her in the past, even though it might not be good for her. Yet, rather than looking back on her experiences with anger, she has learned to make friends with them.

Paul, 45

Paul was sexually abused by his mother from a young age until he left home at fourteen to go to boarding school. Upon returning home for holidays, continuing for many years, he was subjected to continuing abuse. He and his siblings lived under constant threat of their mother's illness. If they failed to do what was expected, she would become ill and have to be hospitalized. They children were made to know that it was their fault.

Paul began to abuse alcohol and drugs. At thirty he married for the first time, seventeen-year-old girl. The marriage lasted a few years until his young wife could no longer stand the constant stress of his substance abuse. He had emotional affairs with married women who fell for his charm and good looks.

Diagnosed with bulimia and borderline personality disorder, which is unusual for a male, Paul had a habit of cutting himself. By the time he was thirty-five he had made numerous suicide attempts and had been admitted to hospitals more than 20 times for mental health issues.

It was not until he was late into his thirties that he finally met a therapist who was able to help him open up begin to deal with his sexual and substance abuse issues. While he the struggle continued for many years, he eventually fell in love and has maintained the relationship over a long period of time.

Reproduction interdite

Paul's handwriting is artistic and creative—he is a talented artist and sculptor. Yet, the brittleness of the stroke reveals his sensitivity and extreme emotional fragility at the time of writing.

The covering stroke on the printed "a" is frequently found in samples written by survivors of sexual abuse and indicates the difficulty the writer has in expressing his or her feelings about the abuse. Why? The a is in the middle zone and is particular to communication. The covering stroke gives the writer a place to hide and avoid talking about painful subjects.

The lack of ligatures and jumpy rhythm suggest that under stress Paul has few emotional resources on which to call, so at the time of writing there was a tendency to fall apart and/or fall back on alcohol for support.

The thick line of ink produces dark strokes known as "pastosity," which refers to a doughy, pasta-like quality often seen in the handwriting of artists and those who live close to the earth. Writing with a felt-tipped pen requires little effort to produce a pastose line. The writer enjoys the "good things" in life but wants them to come easily to him. He may work hard but would prefer not to if at all possible.

Perhaps one of the most important aspects of Paul's handwriting sample is the lowercase (unconscious area) letter "g", which is made in three separate parts. The separations in the "g" attest to an inability at the time of writing for him to integrate his sexuality with his everyday life. The loops on the lower parts of the "g" are inflated like a balloon. Large loops are containers for emotion and imagination, in this case, since they are in the lower zone, they have to do specifically with sex. However, when there are exaggerations they point to problem areas. In the lower zone, inflated loops indicate a lack of emotional satisfaction.

The overall handwriting is "form conscious," which means that more attention is given to the way things look than to the message itself. Form conscious writers can't stand it if anyone sees them as less than perfect. Their fear that they are, in fact, less than perfect, is hidden behind the protective façade of their unique letter designs.

Two sisters from a dysfunctional family

The father, who is described by various family members as "weak, pathetic, and feminine," sexually abused his son and three daughters. The son was nine years old when he awoke to find his father fondling him.

After sniffing cleaning fluid, the youngest daughter was rushed to the hospital in cardiac arrest at the age of thirteen and died. Her alcoholic mother, blamed another of the daughters, Jeanine, because Jeanine had known what her sister was doing and kept quiet about it.

Two months after the girl's death, the father killed himself with a gunshot to the head. The son grew up to be a religious fanatic who refuses to allow his mother and sisters to talk about their younger sibling's death.

The children, raised with little supervision, were described as spoiled, obnoxious, and rude. In their forties, Jeanine and Cynthia had a reputation as shoplifters and party girls. Both have had DWI citations.

Cynthia, 41

Cynthia was a teenager when her mother discovered her having sex with her brother. Despite dealing with chronic alcoholism, Cynthia has managed to hold a steady job working for the government. Typically, her relationships have been short-lived. One marriage ended in divorce in less than a year.

Cynthia's handwriting is too crowded for its large size. People who have a need to control all space fear that if they let go, everything will fall apart. The handwriting has strong regularity, which adds to the need for control.

She puts herself first in all things and makes sure that her needs are met before anyone else is considered. The form of the PPI she uses is far removed from what Cynthia learned in school.

Although basically a "Roman PPI," which is somewhat unusual in a cursive writing, the hooks at the beginnings of the top and bottom crossbars indicate anger and resentment toward both parents. Yet, the curved form of the bar indicates a "caving in," so that, despite the negative feelings, she accepts them.

21

> I am an A[...] [...] in [...]
> Insurance Claims
> department. I have two dogs
> named [...] and S[...]. I bought
> my first house about two years
> ago. I'm at my mom's house writing
> this. I'm writing this for [...]

There are numerous sharp angles where they don't belong, such as on the tops of "m's" which point to unexpressed emotions. This is in conflict with the large size, which reveals her freedom in expressing her emotions. The apparent contradiction is resolved when we understand that Cynthia is emotive, but not when it comes to her deeper feelings, which she cannot directly discuss.

The t-crosses that bow in the middle are sometimes referred to as the "victim t," made by someone with a poor self-image who frequently puts herself in a position to be punished.

Many of Cynthia's upper loops are pointed at the apex. More often than not, such pointed upper loops are the result of a blow to the head. They reflect unrealistic, twisted thinking. Her idiosyncratic worldview does not conform with reality.

A letter design that appears in Cynthia's handwriting is frequently seen in the handwritings of adults who were raised in a family where alcoholism was a family secret. This is the letters "a" and/or "o" that are completely encircled before it goes forward (called the "double-joined oval"). Since alcoholic families are complicit in keeping family secrets, the kids are taught to "talk around" emotional situations without ever really confronting them.

Jeanine, 43

A promiscuous alcoholic and drug abuser who has a reputation as a pathological liar, acquaintances report that Jeanine lives in a bad part of town in a home overrun by vermin. Her young son gets in trouble at school so often that the state threatened to remove him from her custody.

Jeanine's handwriting, like her sister's, is large and crowded, but with more rounded forms, which shows less need for control and a greater need for approval. The odd-shaped PPI with its overblown lower loop (father figure) demonstrates her unmet need for approval, attention, and affection from men, which leads to promiscuous behavior.

The writing leans slightly to the left (see the beginning strokes on "h"), which is movement away from the right side of the paper. The right side represents father and authority figures. Like her sister, Jeanine makes double-joined ovals, where the stroke goes all the way around the letter before moving forward, revealing an inability to directly discuss emotional issues. Most letters return to the baseline, which is symbolic of needing to have both feet on the ground. Such a writer is pragmatic and experiences the world through her concrete senses. Philosophical conversation quickly bores her to distraction.

Jeanine is highly sociable and indiscriminate in her choice of friends. The writing has an overall slack rhythm, which indicates low willpower in someone who is easily persuaded to do things that she knows are bad for her. She takes the easy way whenever possible and has an emotional age of about 15.

Some of the forms in this sample, like the number "6" on line 4, have a snakelike appearance, which may be seen in the handwritings of relentlessly manipulative clients. Jeanine might be diagnosed as having Borderline Personality Disorder.

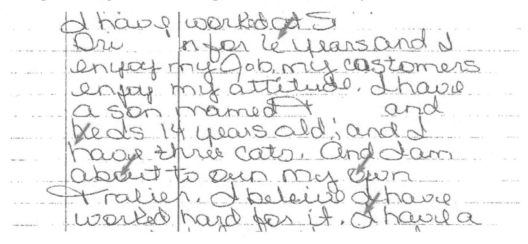

Diana, 51

Raped in her teens by boys she thought were her friends, as an adult Diana continues to be traumatized by the experience. She developed an eating disorder, then an addiction to cigarettes and pot, which she subsequently conquered. She has long suffered from chronic depression which has improved at times and then exacerbated again. She has threatened suicide many times and is known to have hoarded drugs and antidepressants.

Diana dresses only in trousers, claiming that her legs are ugly. She wears only black when she goes out. It is her stated belief that most males as sexually attracted to her. During intercourse, she refuses to have a light on or allow her partner to see her naked. Her romantic illusions and delusions have led her to indulge in unrealistic fantasies about a man she was in love with. When he married someone else, Diana threatened suicide.

At the clinic where she works, Diana is known as an extremely conscientious employee who is anxious to "do right." She arrives on time, completes her work on time, and performs well in family counseling, as well as in patient education and drug counseling. The problem is that her attitudes toward patients and staff can change without warning.

The masculine appearance of Diana's handwriting indicates discomfort with her sexuality. Poor rhythm and fluctuation in letter design (form), which switches between printing and cursive writing, are hallmarks of anxious, emotionally labile and unpredictable people. Acting one way in a given situation, she will respond differently under similar circumstances next time, doing what feels good at the moment, appropriate or not.

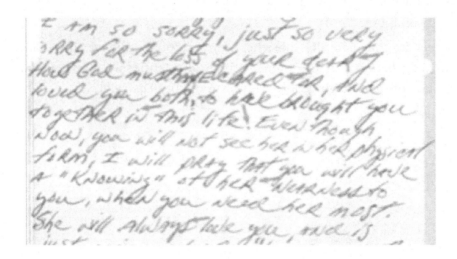

The space between letters is also variable, and the word spacing is made too narrow by the very long, curved end strokes that reach out at the end of a word in many cases, to touch the beginning of the next word. This lack of respect for social boundaries leads Diana to crowd others and invade their space. She is indiscriminate in her choice of friends, seeing quantity as more attractive than quality. Keeping many people around her may make her feel protected.

When letters grow larger at the ends of words, the writer literally must have the last word. She sometimes presents herself as less forceful and intimidating, then, comes on strong when you least expect it and refuses to back down. Capital letters mid-word, plus variable pressure pattern with sudden darker areas of ink, add to the picture of unpredictable and possibly explosive behavior.

Her signature, not shown here for privacy reasons, is congruent with the text. The heavy "i" dots and punctuation are a sign of perseveration often seen in the handwritings of abuse victims who have been unable to resolve their issues. The fluctuation in Diana's moods and behavior might lead to a diagnosis of Borderline Personality Disorder.

Adam 70

As a child, Adam was sexually abused by an older brother for more than eight years, while he secretly enjoyed what he knew was unacceptable to his parents. After he married and had two children, Adam began to frequent adult book stores and gay bars, at the same time preaching and teaching strict morality.

His secret life continued for some time, with a growing addiction to pornography that started with videos and magazines, and later made easier by the Internet. His wife, upon discovering his activities, insisted he join a recovery group, which helped for a limited amount of time.

While Adam is highly intelligent, having several advanced degrees and authoring books and programs for religious groups, his addiction to gay porn, especially that featuring young boys, eventually took over every spare moment of his life. He had difficulty even communicating with his family.

Diagnosed in therapy as a narcissist, Adam seemed unable to understand why his wife finally demanded that he leave the home. Eventually, worried about Adam's physical health and accepting his promises to stop the pornography, his wife took him back. Within a few months she caught him repeating the behavior. Upon her final ultimatum to either get help or leave the house for good, Adam began to attend a church ministry.

Over time, he supposedly changed his views toward pornography and homosexuality. His wife reports that he became less denigrating of women and has made an effort to be more open and less narcissistic and angry.

Adam's handwriting has a somewhat feminine quality in its softness and emphasis on movement. The ink stroke (ductus) is thick and sensuous, which denotes a writer who is easily aroused by anything that excites the concrete senses, especially tactile sensations. He wants more of everything, whatever it is–brighter colors, spicier foods, perhaps; louder music. The "finer things in life." He is profoundly affected by that which is natural–the scent of wood smoke in the morning; walking barefoot on a sandy beach. Artificial flowers or cheap perfume would leave him cold.

The writing becomes more threadlike (indefinite letter forms) and harder to read as it continues down the page and Adam becomes more enthusiastic about his subject. The words are written fairly close together, but not unreasonably so, showing moderate social needs. Yet, the slant moves in all directions, indicating his conflicting feelings about social interaction.

His intelligence is revealed in the speed of the writing and its simplified forms, which demonstrate an ability to cut out the non-essential parts of an issue and get to the bottom line. Combining letters, such as the "t-h" connection in the word "then", sixth line down, indicates a capacity of quick thinking and skill in creating new ways of doing things, rather than relying on standard tried-and-true methods.

The letter forms tend to break down and become illegible, which tells us that his thoughts

are clearer than his verbal communications. He might say something that can be interpreted multiple ways. Or you may come back later and quote him and he'll say, "but that's not what I meant." In other words, he prevaricates.

The t-crossing in the word "to" in the sixth line is made with a slashing motion that points to quick temper and hostility acted out (the "dominating t-bar"). In the fourth line, first word, "showing," the letter "g" is left open at the bottom, so that it looks more like an "x". Writers who adopt these types of forms have sometimes experienced the loss of a relationship. It's as if the bottom has fallen out of their love life. Several instances of the letter "p" have a phallic appearance and may be unconsciously related to fantasies involving the penis.

John, 50

Raised by a single mother who spent more time on church activities than raising her children, John was sexually assaulted at the age of nine by an older boy in the church. In order to prove his manhood, he married a much older woman as soon as he turned 18. After a subsequent divorce, had numerous short-term relationships and two more marriages.

Never having received treatment for the early abuse, nor several other major traumas that have occurred over his lifetime, John has long masked social phobia and panic attacks with alcohol and some early drug use. In his late forties, on the heels of a series of shocking deaths of close family members and friends, followed by the painful loss of the business he had worked hard to build, John collapsed and was hospitalized suffering from a serious potassium deficiency. When he returned home, he was struck with sudden and severe agoraphobia, which impacted every area of his life.

John's handwriting has changed a great deal over a period of years, going from highly connected with a strong rightward trend, indicating an ability to interact with others, to its current small-size staccato (jumpy) printing.

This highly simplified writing with its sharp dashed i-dots demonstrates John's creativity, intellect, and originality. The i-dots are actually slashes which, combined with other sharp angles, such as the "g" in "handwriting" on the second line, are adopted by clever people who use sarcasm as a defense.

disease — a common opinion of handwriting experts who look for all sorts of minute "ticks" on the page.

But if this is her diagnoses, she will at least be partially correct.

The "tick" was caused by excessive sa

The small size of the writing and wide word spacing suggest a shy person who would rather be alone or with one or two familiar people than a crowd. The slight threadiness of the printing plus some right slant reveals one who is able to use great charm and wit when forced to interact with others. Any type of social interaction, leaves him overstimulated and anxious.

The baseline bounces along, moving up and down, but not too much. This is a lively, fun-loving individual, but the wide spaces between words and the cut-off lower loops show how very careful he is about whom he allows into his inner circle. As with many of the samples above, the "g's" and "y's" are left hanging below the baseline, demonstrating his inability to address his past sexual issues.

John's feelings toward his mother, who failed to protect him, range from hostility and pity. The cradled "g" in "diagnoses" is symbolic of searching for "mother," or what mothering traditionally represents: nurturing and care-taking, but not finding it.

28

The Addictive Personality
and its Handwriting

By Sheila Lowe

The Addictive Personality

© 1997 by Sheila R. Lowe

sheila@sheilalowe.com

www.sheilalowe.com

All rights reserved. No portion of this book may be reproduced, by any process or technique, without the express written consent of the author, except small excerpts, for purpose of review.

Pain is a shared experience

When you think of an addict, what comes to mind? Someone unkempt, ragged, homeless perhaps, eyes burning feverishly with the desperate need for the next fix — the "fix" being the addict's drug of choice—heroin, speed, PCP, alcohol? Most people tend to categorize addicts that way.

Addiction, however, is not the exclusive province of drug users and alcoholics. It encompasses a far greater range of behaviors than simply the ingestion of various toxic substances; and it crosses cultural, racial, gender, age, and most other boundaries. The key word is "behaviors." Anything one does to excess can become an addition. Television can be addictive. Shopping can be addictive. Sex, food, cigarettes, religion, gambling can be addictive; exercise, video games, or work can be addictive. The Internet can be addictive.

In fact, addiction may be associated with any substance, artifact, or behavior which, when its natural use is perverted, transmutes normal functioning into a downward spiraling process, too often ending in destruction.

Unfortunately, the addict's behavior destroys not only himself. Along the way, his self-esteem, career, social status, health, financial standing and self-respect may be lost. But in addition, the entire family structure is likely to collapse under the weight of the all-consuming drive to satisfy his habit. What probably began as a pleasurable activity eventually turns into a nightmare.

The metamorphosis is so gradual, so subtle, that it may be some time before the addict realizes that every waking moment is spent serving the addiction. One day he wakes up and nothing else matters but the drug or behavior that makes him feel good. His time, money, and energy are expended on obtaining the exhilaration that comes from the high.

Coping with Pain

Something all humans share is that we are forced to face painful events at one time or another. One may suffer loss, rejection, humiliation, unkindness, and many other unpleasant common experiences. Being fired from a job, discovering that one's spouse is having an affair, or the death of a parent, for example, produce painful emotions that must somehow be dealt with.

Various defenses can be called into play to handle emotional pain and help one cope. The coping mechanism of choice depends very much on personality type. Some find comfort in talking things through with friends or a therapist, while others prefer to be left alone in their sadness.

Some throw themselves into work, some eat, some withdraw, going to sleep for long periods, or use alcohol, tranquilizers, or a host of other activities and substances. In fact, anything that makes one feel better could be considered a coping or defense mechanism.

Needing a bit of help to get through the bad times is absolutely normal and reasonable. During the time when the need is most extreme, defenses can be healthy and appropriate. Emotional growth may even result from the suffering and make it a little more palatable. However, one who leans on a defense until it becomes a crutch, and then refuses to give it up once the situation is resolved, is asking for serious trouble.

Because winning at gambling, shopping for bargains, or eating a bowl of ice-cream; or being anesthetized by alcohol or drugs made him feel so much better, the suffering person learns to trust the good feeling. He wants to bring the feeling back, again and again and again. While performing the addictive behavior of choice—gambling, drinking, shopping, or whatever it may be—every bit of his attention and energy his focused on the pleasure obtained from being "buzzed." This serves to create an acceptable distance between the addict and his pain.

The pleasurable mood change produced by the addictive behavior is a constant, something he can count on as a source of pleasure when other parts of his life are not working well. He may at first resist acting out the behavior, but as the pain returns and intensifies he turns to it more and more.

The irony is, the sufferer uses the behavior to relieve pain, but the more he uses it, the more he relies upon it, and the less able he is to properly deal with his problems. As he has increasing trouble dealing with his problems, he turns more and more to the source of relief. A vicious cycle has begun.

They all serve the same purpose

Addictive behaviors are many and diverse, almost unlimited; but a common thread seems to bind them together—they allow the sufferer to numb painful feelings and avoid having to face emotional stressors. They serve to help him ignore the guilt or shame that plague him while he is not acting out. The relief, though, is only temporary.

Most addictive behaviors have socially acceptable uses. There is nothing inherently bad in drinking a glass or two of wine, it produces a pleasant glow. But when the glass becomes five or six or twelve on a consistent basis the normal use of the substance is twisted into something harmful.

Similarly, eating a bowl of ice cream feels good and is probably okay. Eating a half-gallon of chocolate fudge night after night, on the other hand, changes the acceptable use of a treat into a damaging activity with potential for serious negative consequences.

Some addictions are more obvious than others. For instance, a drunk driver is not as difficult to identify as is a compulsive shopper. Let's say you see a car weaving in and out of traffic, crossing the white line and nearly crashing into other cars. The common reaction is, "Is he drunk, or what?!" The compulsive shopper, carrying an armload of packages from a department store is unlikely to draw any attention. Yet, the spending addiction is just as real and can be just as destructive as the alcoholic's habit.

Even pleasure in and of itself can be addictive. In a 1950's experiment, scientists at the Montreal Neurological Institute implanted electrodes in the brains of laboratory rats. The rats were taught to press a lever which stimulated the pleasure center of their brains.

Once the rats discovered that the enjoyable sensations they experienced came from pressing the lever, some of them began returning to it time and time again, pressing the lever until they passed out from exhaustion. They began stimulating themselves more and more in order to get the good feeling continuously. Soon the rats were pressing the lever to the exclusion of any other activity, including eating, sex, or sleeping. They eventually stimulated themselves to death.

The addict is not so different from those lab rats. Once hooked on the behavior or substance that provides the desired shot of euphoria, he returns to it again and again until he is virtually unable to withdraw from doing it. In a desperate search for relief from pain through pleasure (or at least numbing the pain), he keeps on "pressing the lever" more and more, until he is as good as dead. Or is actually dead.

As the compulsion to cling to the behavior, artifact, or substance grows, other people become less important in the addict's life. Somewhere along the way, personal relationships start to assume less importance because they are not as predictable as the mood change that comes with the addictive behavior. The addict knows where to turn for consistent comfort. The behavior or substance will not let him down. Sadly, his sense of serenity is based on a lie and cannot last.

What does the mood change do?

The mood change allows the addict to detach and distance himself from pain and a sense of hopelessness. It fills up the emptiness and erroneously leads him to believe he is in control of his circumstances. And control is extremely important to him.

The mood change allows him to avoid unpleasant realities. Performing the behavior or using the substance feels so much better than the reality that the addict becomes dependent upon it to feel good. Consequently, he is drawn into a cycle of escalating need to act out more and more in order to experience the same level of euphoria that he first enjoyed.

Interestingly, the book, *The Three Pound Universe* notes, "People don't self-stimulate constantly—as long as they're feeling good. Only when they're depressed does the stimulation trigger a big response."

"Addictive personality" in handwriting?

Craig Nakken writes in *The Addictive Personality* that the addictive personality does not exist before the addiction but is created from the illness. He calls addictions an "impulse-control disorder." For the graphologist, the question is, can the "addictive personality" be identified in handwriting?

Although the characteristics of dependency are present in handwriting to one degree or another, it is not possible to predict the type of addiction that the writer is likely to hook into.

Positive family relationships in childhood teach us how to reach out and touch others. By engaging in an interchange of ideas, feelings, and experiences, even young children learn to acquire the skills needed for nurturing others. They also discover how to receive nurturing and love. In other words, they learn how to connect.

In a healthy family, the child learns first how to love and nurture himself by following his mother and other family members' example. He is taught to depend on other family members and become an integral part of the whole. He grows up knowing how it feels to be needed and that is it appropriate to help others. At the same time, he learns that it is to okay to accept help when it is his turn.

When a crisis arises, he is able to go within and call on his personal resources for strength. A sense of responsibility for self and others develops, and he learns to look at the big picture, not just his own circumstances.

The child is thus equipped to enter the community and develop diverse, interdependent relationships. He welcomes change rather than resisting it because he has confidence in his capacity to adopt alternative paths.

Change is recognized as a vital component of growth.

Addictive relationships result in isolation from others because the addict is unable to sustain nurturing or loving behavior over a long period of time. He views personal relationships as useful only as long as they serve the addiction. Interactions with others tend to be superficial and one way—his way. Addictive relationships break the connections with others.

Susceptibility to addiction is often found in those who grew up in families where there was little or no connection or closeness, or worse, interaction between family members was chaotic and unhealthy. Learning how to form wholesome relationships was not part of the curriculum. Trusting others and developing interpersonal skills was outside their realm of experience.

The consequences of addiction encompass many aspects of life; however, these can all be reduced to two major areas of functioning: Relationships and impulse control. Three dominant personality characteristics common to the addictive personality, and which can be identified in handwriting, are fear of intimacy, avoidance of reality, and lack of impulse control. These can be seen in handwriting:

> **Fear of intimacy** - *Disturbed picture of space (extra-wide spaces between words, sometimes "rivers"). Wide letter and word spacing, narrow left margin, wide right margin, small middle zone, many abrupt disconnections, narrow middle zone, word endings long and straight or abruptly cut off.*

> **Avoidance of reality** - *Disturbed picture of form or form-conscious, "persona" writing style; inability to maintain a steady baseline (avoidance of baseline), wide or variable right margin, variable slant, very light or displaced pressure, intruded ovals, double-joined ovals, ovals with extra loops.*

***Lack of impulse control** - Uneven picture of movement/disturbed rhythm, lower zone emphasis, variable middle zone height, variable lower zone, strong right slant, variable slant, muddy ductus, very heavy or uneven pressure, highly variable right margin. In other words, variability everywhere.*

Family Dynamics Set the Stage

The roots of addiction are found within the family dynamic. In order to understand why some individuals make the choices they do we must examine some of the different structures that provide the soil in which the addictive personality flourishes.

Over the next pages, we will discuss four negative family structures that can be identified by their handwritings, as follows:

- Neglectful and Abusive
- Humiliating and Attacking
- Hostile and Aggressive
- Inconsistent and Unstable

1. Neglectful and Abusive Family Structure

Nurturing behavior is of primary importance for an infant and later child when it comes to developing self-esteem. When his mother shows by her actions, hugging and holding, tone of voice and facial expressions that she loves her child, he feels good about himself. His ego develops properly and he knows on a very basic level that he deserves to take up space in the world.

The child who grows up without being held or touched, except in a hostile, violent way, feels he has no right to live. He becomes passive, dead inside. To avoid feeling the pain of rejection he puts his emotions to sleep. Without the self-assurance of a strong ego, the child feels powerless. He becomes a follower who waits to be told exactly what to do and how to feel. Chronically depressed, he seeks the excitement and false confidence that addictive behaviors engender. Once the high is gone he quickly falls back into depression. Overeating and other oral behaviors (heavy drinking, continual toothpick or gum chewing, nail-biting, talking too much, etc.) may be symptomatic of the neglectful/abusive family structure.

Handwriting characteristics of the child of a neglectful or abusive family structure may include (but are not limited to) the following:

Weak pressure, rounded forms, middle zone emphasis, compact picture of space, disturbed rhythm, downhill or wavy baseline, narrow middle zone, small or short capital letters.

Independence! I think don't understand me my way of thinking are not used to do in

2. Humiliating and Attacking Family Structure

Parents who are too demanding, who seek perfection, and who never give the child credit for his accomplishments teach him that he can never do anything right or be good enough. If he gets an A on his report card, they want to know why he didn't bring home an A+.

Each day when he returns home from school, the child readies himself for battle. He knows that, whatever he does, there will be some reason why it wasn't done well enough. Such negative parental messages produce a profound sadness in him, which he turns inward on himself.

His sadness eventually turns into rage, which he knows he must suppress or suffer the consequences. Continually striving to do better, to be perfect, to win approval from those in authority, deep inside, he knows that nothing he does will be good enough.

Frustration seethes beneath the surface as he fears that if people "really" knew him, they would not like him. This is often the case in a home where religious fanaticism exists and leads to an overly controlling adult.

Handwriting characteristics of the child of an attacking or humiliating family structure may include (but are not limited to) the following:

Overall rigidity and narrowness; tall, retraced upper zone, angular forms, crowded picture of space, heavy pressure. Emphasis is on contraction, rather than the balance that comes with release.

*"My ideal work environment is one w.
...ery professional; yet sensitive to person...
...I enjoy a work environment that is ope...
ideas and communicates information rec...*

3. Hostile and Aggressive Family Structure

Parents who use their child either as a sexual object or a punching bag on whom to take out their frustrations send the message that only their own needs are important. The child's right to nurturing, protection and love is shoved aside in favor of the adult's selfish desires.

Whether the abuse is physical, emotional, or sexual, the victimized child learns that he must give up—literally, his Self. His job is to stand by passively and wait for the parent(s) to act out their impulses on him.

By watching his parents' aggressive, impulsive behavior, he learns two important lessons: 1) it is acceptable to do whatever you feel like doing, no matter how much it hurts other people. 2) it is not safe to trust others. After all, if you cannot trust your parents, who can you trust?

This type of family structure seems especially prone to breed cocaine and other types of antisocial drug use. Handwriting characteristics of the child of a hostile and aggressive family structure may include (but are not limited to) the following:

> *Disturbed movement, especially in the lower zone (i.e., overblown, detached or twisted lower loops;) disturbed form (i.e., strong variability in the middle zone), arcade forms, elaboration.*

*looking for a man wh...
...nately share this and...
...ugh my beliefs are con...
...I find it limiting to...
...truth," I think these...*

4. Inconsistent and Unstable Family Structure

Consistency and stability are very important components in developing a child's mental and emotional health. Growing up in a chaotic home where the rules are continually changing teaches the child that you cannot count on anyone or anything.

For instance, when a child witnesses one parent striking the other, and then denies having done so, the child feels as if he must be crazy, because "parents don't lie." He knows what he saw, but how could it be real, if the parent says it didn't happen?

When a parent behaves in a loving, caring manner one minute, then turns around and screams at the child or beats him the next, the child never knows what to expect or what will set the parent off.

The child learns that what he sees and feels cannot be real, that he cannot trust his own feelings and that he cannot trust others. He is in a double bind and suffers from a dichotomy of needs. Deeply lonely, he cannot trust others enough to allow intimacy. His desperate need for closeness and parental love can never fully be satisfied because his parents simply are not emotionally and/or physically available to him. Handwriting characteristics of the child of an inconsistent and unstable family structure may include (but are not limited to) the following:

Secondary expansion, combination of garland/thread forms, wide loops, elaborate capital letters, large overall size, arrhythmic movement with emphasis on release.

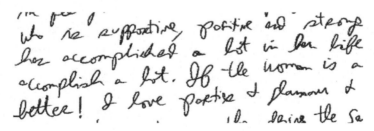

Common Characteristics of Dysfunctional Families

In exploring these four types of unhealthy, dysfunctional families, we find several commonalities. In all of these family structures the child learns:

> ➢ *not to trust himself or others*
> ➢ *his needs are unimportant*
> ➢ *to react to external events, not his own feelings*
> ➢ *he is powerless*
> ➢ *to fear intimacy despite his need for closeness*
> ➢ *not to believe reality*
> ➢ *impulsive behavior is acceptable*

➤ *abusive behavior is acceptable*

The elements that comprise the development of the addictive personality run the gamut. Conditions in the environment, heredity, sensitivity, one's personal experiences and his reactions to them all play their part. Children from dysfunctional homes do not always grow up to develop addictive personalities, but these harmful family structures are typical breeding grounds for the attitudes and behavior that spawn addiction.

Those with a healthier family history are far more likely to seek consistency and predictability in their relationships and familiar situations when under stress. They know they can turn to family and friends for support, and do not need the crutch provided by alcohol, drugs, or other addictive behaviors.

The addictive person, however, draws comfort from his ritualized behavior, even when it brings more of the pain that he tries so assiduously to deny. He operates within different parameters from the average person.

When faced with emotional challenges, such as relationship problems, he takes an "I don't need you" attitude and turns inward, seeking solace in his particular choice of chemical or behavior, rather than turning to another individual.

The sex addict who is stressed on the job may not turn to alcohol for relief but seeks a new sexual partner for the night. The computer addict who doesn't want to face her impending divorce spends eighteen hours a day, gaming on the Internet. The alcoholic who is having trouble with his boss downs another beer. The wife who is worried about finances goes shopping for another new outfit she doesn't need.

After performing the addiction ritual, the addict often feels ashamed. His self-respect suffers and he sees himself as more and more powerless. The weaker he feels, the more he seeks to hide from it. Eventually, like the lab rats, he begins to live only for the moment, taking comfort in the predictability of the mood change he experiences when acting out.

In his lonely lifestyle, addiction becomes the primary relationship. It becomes more and more difficult to develop and sustain nourishing involvements over the long-term. He begins to rely on the high to get by day to day, even though he may hate himself for the dependency.

Like Dr. Jekyll and Mr. Hyde, the addict's personality alters over time and he may begin to feel like Dr. Jekyll in this passage from the Robert Louis Stevenson book:

"...whereas in the beginning the difficulty had been to throw off the body of Jekyll, it had of late gradually but decidedly transferred itself to the other side. I was slowly losing hold of my original and better self and becoming slowly incorporated with my second and worse self."

As the different areas of his life become affected, the addict develops additional destructive coping mechanisms, which generally include denial (that he has a problem), lying (about his activities), and rationalizing (that his miserable situation is everyone else's fault).

> *The food addict may begin hiding food*
> *The sex addict may begin going to prostitutes*
> *The gambling addict may open a secret bank account or get a secret second job*
> *The alcoholic may begin secretly drinking on his way home from work*

All of these behaviors, as well as other addictive behaviors, have an interesting element in common—they are performed secretly, independently, alone. They serve to further reinforce the addict's belief that he does not need anyone. Yet, while he rejects the advances of other people, at the same time, he feels hurt and angry when they withdraw from him. However, the constant fear that "this episode" of acting out is the one that will make 'them' leave him is not as strong as the desire for the mood change.

In handwriting we might look for these defenses in the "communication area," such as oval letters obscured by extra loops, hooks, or other intrusions:

As the addiction gains a stronger hold, the addict's behavior becomes increasingly self-centered. The time and energy he once devoted to loved ones and friends is now absorbed by acting out the addiction. He is no longer interested in the things that once made him happy—his child's happy laughter, a walk along the beach at sunset with his wife, dining out with friends. The anesthetizing effect of the addiction is all that matters.

His attitude says...

> *I don't need anyone else*
> *I don't have to face anything unpleasant if I don't want to*
> *I can do whatever I want to, no matter who it hurts*

The problem is, the very nature of addiction ultimately causes the process to break down. The euphoria finally fails him and life is now just a gaping wound that hurts all the time. Nakken suggests that a progressive breakdown occurs in the addict's life as he tests his boundaries at work and at home, with the following results.

Living skills collapse

Reasoning skills collapse He begins to avoid whatever does not serve the addiction, which includes any unfamiliar or new situation or relationships. This produces a rigid, unsociable lifestyle which prevents forward movement and growth.

Coping skills collapse His inability to resolve issues or handle stress provides an excuse to increasingly act out. He needs the addictive substance or behavior just to function in ordinary life situations.

Emotional controls collapse Heightened emotional tension causes fits of rage to erupt for no apparent reason. There may be uncontrollable crying jags and a feeling that everyone is out to get him. He projects his guilt onto others, attacking them before he can be attacked.

Interpersonal skills collapse Feelings of insecurity about interacting with others intensify, goading him to attach himself to objects or events, rather than other people. He begins to believe that others can see right through him—and all too often they can. His shame and guilt make transparent that which he tries to hide.

Need for power and control

Addiction has everything to do with power and control. The addict makes his own rules and does not concern himself about how they affect others. He is willing to intimidate and manipulate the people around him in order to have things his way. Weakness is intolerable. He must be in control, he must be right. He may appear calm on the surface, but inside he suffers from instability and low self-esteem. Knowing that he has the power in his relationships gives him some sense of security, so being challenged by his partner is out of the question. Any attempts at independence on the part of his mate are likely to be met with outbursts of rage.

Addiction produces nothing good or positive. It is a degenerative process. The addict's satisfaction is derived from external pursuits, rather than from spiritual values or interaction with other people. Living for the moment, having intense experiences, makes him feel more real, more alive. To feel good, he needs to blot out reality and help him forget his troubles. Once the pleasure of the addictive substance or behavior fades, however, he does not hesitate to cast aside the person or object that helped him create the mood change and go on to something or someone else that looks more exciting.

The Healthy Personality

Sensuality and materialistic pursuits fill one up on merely a conscious level, leaving a gaping spiritual vacuum. Indulging in excesses of one kind or another all the time will eventually leave one feeling bored and depressed. The body, mind and soul need some relief, some type of feeding beyond all pleasure, all the time.

The healthy personality is able to enjoy pleasure without abusing it. He learns from his experiences and relationships and wants to grow from them. His coping skills are used only when appropriate, and he is not frightened by change. Painful incidents do not crush him emotionally, but he is able to work through them and move on. He is able to provide love and support to others, with a give-and-take attitude. He makes intimate connections without difficulty.

The healthy personality cultivates a support system which includes a positive self-image and interpersonal relationships. It incorporates a balance of several elements:

- *Self-respect*
- *Self-esteem*
- *Self-confidence*
- *Self-discipline*
- *Self-control*
- *Self-determination*
- *Self-importance*
- *Self-love*

The healthy personality does not blindly follow the childlike compulsion to do whatever feels good, right now, without regard to the consequences. He exercises reasonable control over his impulses and listens to his conscience. He is not controlled by the coping or defense mechanisms he chooses. When he feels conflicted his self-discipline usually wins out and he is not controlled by the defense.

The healthy personality cares about himself and others. He knows it is wrong to hurt people and makes an effort to treat others with dignity. He takes responsibility for his choices and does not try to blame circumstances, events, or other people for his mistakes.

By cultivating positive relationships with self, family and friends, within the community, and within a spiritual belief system, the healthy person gets important feedback about what he is projecting about who he is. He learns how to give and to receive, to see how his behavior affects others and how he is affected by them. He learns how to lean on himself and develop his inner resources; to accept change and work with it; to make goals, rather than just living for the moment.

Perhaps most importantly, he sees himself as part of the world community, rather than as a solitary being in a sea of nothingness. Healthy relationships consist of give-and-take, which means reaching out to others and interacting with them; making a connection. Failing that ability, one turns to other sources of support where the "give" aside is put aside and only "take" remains in the isolation produced by addictive behavior.

There are countless books and self-help groups who deal effectively with recovery. Nonetheless, it may be helpful to review a brief listing of some of the skills the addict will need to develop as he moves along the road to emotional, physical and spiritual health:

> *Develop positive coping skills*
> *Learn to tolerate, even welcome, change*
> *Develop a good conscience*
> *Learn to reach out to others*
> *Learn to abandon controlling behaviors*
> *Learn to form positive relationships*
> *Learn to use power kindly*
> *Learn not to abuse pleasurable pursuits*
> *Develop spiritual values*
> *Learn not to be afraid of life's challenges*
> *Learn to live in the moment, not for the moment*

Characteristics of the Healthy Personality

✓ *Ability to love and nurture self*
✓ *Does not avoid uncomfortable feelings*
✓ *Welcomes and accepts change*
✓ *Healthy interdependencies others are important*
✓ *Accepts responsibility*
✓ *Comfortable setting long-term goals Strong sense of self-esteem*
✓ *Self-discipline*
✓ *Self-respect*

Characteristics of Healthy Relationships

✓ *Nurturing*
✓ *Provide love, emotional growth*
✓ *Give-and-take*
✓ *Based on emotional connection*

Steps to Addiction

✓ *Experimentation seeking the mood change through external means*
✓ *Usage begins to seek the mood change regularly*
✓ *Dependence needs the mood change to function normally*

Symptoms of Addiction

- ✓ *Loss of control over the behavior*
- ✓ *Compulsion to act out*
- ✓ *Continued behavior despite negative consequences*
- ✓ *Social relationships are affected*

Coping Mechanisms of the Addict

- ➢ *Denial ("I don't have a problem")*
- ➢ *Repression ("forgets" bad behavior)*
- ➢ *Lying ("No, I didn't drink on the way home")*
- ➢ *Rationalization ("I hold down a good job, pay my bills. Why shouldn't I enjoy life?")*

Excuses for acting out

- ➢ *Feeling powerless*
- ➢ *Feeling weak*
- ➢ *Feeling helpless*

When Tolerance Develops

- ➢ *Mood change isn't enough*
- ➢ *Acts out more often, more dangerously*
- ➢ *Old pleasures mean little now*
- ➢ *Constant stress*
- ➢ *Is in pain all the time*
- ➢ *Avoids anything unfamiliar*
- ➢ *Inability to control emotional reactions*
- ➢ *Insecure interacting with others*
- ➢ *Thinks of nothing but acting out*

Characteristics of Addictive Relationships

- ✓ *Non-nurturing*
- ✓ *One-way*
- ✓ *Superficial*
- ✓ *Based on emotional isolation*

Addict's behavior in relationships

- ✓ *Manipulates others*
- ✓ *Self-centered, self-righteous*
- ✓ *Feels like a victim*
- ✓ *Attacks others*
- ✓ *Withdraws from relationships*
- ✓ *Prefers interacting with objects or events instead of people*

Handwriting indicators of the addictive personality

UZ hooks, roundedness, slackness	Strong signs of orality
Wide right margin	Difficulty facing the future, associations
Lack of sufficient horizontal movement	Difficulty facing the future or planning ahead
Rigidity or slackness	Lack of good personal rhythm
Narrow letters with wide word spacing	Independent, doesn't want to count on others
Poor lower zone	Problems with emotional development
Poor middle zone forms	Problems with emotional release, ego
Form breaks down in mz	Inability to cope with daily life
Excessive speed	Poor impulse control
Malformed PPI	Poor male or female image, poor ego
Reversed PPI	Reversal of roles of mother and father
Avoidance of baseline from LZ return strokes	Hesitates to face unconscious urges
Difficulty in maintaining a steady baseline	Emotional lability
Disturbed picture of movement	Mood swings, poor distribution of energy
Disturbed spatial arrangement	Immaturity and low self-image

Diagnostic Criteria for Substance Dependence (may also be applied to other addictive behaviors)

A maladaptive pattern of substance use, leading to clinically significant impairment or distress, as manifested by three (or more) of the following, occurring at any time in the same twelve-month period:

(1) tolerance, as defined by either of the following: a need for markedly increased amounts of the substance to achieve intoxication or desired effect. markedly diminished effect with continued use of the same amount of the substance.

(2) withdrawal, as manifested by either of the following: the characteristic withdrawal syndrome for the substance the same (or a closely related substance) is taken to relieve or avoid withdrawal symptoms.

(3) the substance is often taken in larger amounts or over a longer period than was intended.

(4) there is a persistent desire or unsuccessful efforts to cut down or control substance use.

(5) a great deal of time is spent in activities necessary to obtain the substance (e.g., visiting multiple doctors or driving long distances), use the substance (e.g., chain-smoking) or recover from its effects.

(6) important social, occupational, or recreational activities are given up or reduced because of substance use.

(7) the substance use is continued despite knowledge of having a persistent or recurrent physical or psychological problem that is likely to have been caused or exacerbated by the substance (e.g., current cocaine use despite recognition of cocaine-induced depression or continued drinking despite recognition that an ulcer was made worse by alcohol consumption.

Quick reference to Diagnostic Criteria from DSM-IV

Coping & Defense Mechanisms

By Sheila R. Lowe, CG

Coping & Defense Mechanisms

1989 by Sheila R. Lowe

© Revised 1997 www.sheilalowe.com

All rights reserved. No portion of this book may be reproduced, by any process or technique, without the express written consent of the author, except small excerpts for purpose of review.

Defense Mechanisms

Everyone alive experiences emotional pain from time to time. It is a simple fact of life. Yet, the way we choose to deal with our pain is as individual as we are.

Some people tackle pain head-on as if to say, "Come on--I'm ready for you!" Some pretend to themselves that they have no pain at all. They cut off the bad feeling before it has a chance to make an impact, and act as if everything were okay. Others push their pain down into the dark recesses of their psyche, then find themselves a prisoner—trapped behind the iron bars of fear.

Inability or unwillingness to face emotional pain or stress calls for the use of defense mechanisms—methods of coping. The defenses we adopt depend very much on our personality makeup and are an outgrowth of our need to manage uncomfortable experiences and feelings. Even as infants we are confronted with emotional pain, and defense mechanisms begin to develop very early in life. When a baby's mealtimes are delayed, or the environment is tense, or the baby is separated from its mother, it must find ways to cope with the unpleasant emotions that result.

When the chosen method proves effective it is likely to be used again and again until it becomes habituated. In the following pages we will explore various methods of dealing with stress and pain.

Reactions to Stress

Maintaining a defense system as a way of coping with stress, unpleasant situations or feelings, requires a continual and enormous output of energy. The human psyche has a finite storehouse of energy that is available for distribution between the various parts of personality (physical, mental, emotional) as needed. Defenses demand large chunks of energy be siphoned off from other, more productive, functions. As a result, the defender may find himself constantly tired, unable to perform with spirit, and losing much of the satisfaction that life has to offer.

Stress affects people differently. Researchers have long wondered why some people under stress experience physical symptoms. They may become hypertensive, have headaches or stomachaches, develop ulcers, or experience asthma attacks. Some forms of cancer have even been linked to stress. Others are unaffected physically.

Substance abuse often emerges as a response to stress. Many people use alcohol, tranquilizers, or recreational drugs to dull the feelings of tension and anxiety that arise from stress at work or pain in their relationships. Of course, dependence on these substances is just as damaging, if not more so, as the stressor itself, and many drugs have dangerous and unpleasant side-effects, which is another good reason for using defenses in moderation.

Anxiety

Anxiety is a result of stress, manifest as a feeling of dread, uneasiness, and impending disaster that we feel compelled to counteract. It is a reaction to internal danger, signaling that one's lifestyle, values and goals are creating more stress than one can cope with. According to the late media psychiatrist Dr. David Viscott anxiety is a fear of loss in the future. When anxiety is not effectively managed it leads to feelings of hurt; anger is a result of hurt; and the hurt, when turned inward, becomes guilt; and guilt becomes depression. The effect of this cycle is a sense of low self-worth.

When anxiety becomes too strong, one's chosen defenses are called into play, resulting in the following benefits:

> *Reduction of emotional conflict*
> *Protection of the Self against its own dangerous impulses*
> *Amelioration of the effect of traumatic experiences*
> *Softening of failure or disappointment*
> *Elimination of clashes between attitudes and reality*
> *A sense of adequacy and personal worth*

So, we can see that defenses have the important function of protecting one from feeling unpleasant or frightening emotions. However, since we cannot heal what we cannot feel, the original pain that caused the feelings is pushed down into the subconscious until, like an unborn fetus, it begins kicking up such a commotion that it can no longer be ignored. How might this happen?

Take the case of Maryanne, a twenty-five-year-old woman who grew up in a reasonably loving family in a small town where she completed college and began a career in accounting. She and her adoptive mother had argued and fought during her growing up years, just as much as the average mother and daughter, but when Maryanne found out at the age of 16 that she was adopted, she immediately concluded that the woman who raised her didn't really care about her at all; that she was "no good."

At age twenty she began an unsuccessful search for her birth mother. Telling herself that she "just wanted to know who she was," she pushed away the underlying hurt of knowing that her mother had given her up and smiled through her pain.

During her college years she began drinking too much and picking up men in bars. The alcohol dampened her emotional pain and when she was in a man's arms she felt loved and protected. At least, until the next day, when he was gone and the emptiness set in again.

At work, there was pressure to perform, so she drank more to relieve the stress. Maryanne began to gain weight; not a lot, but enough to make her feel fat and undesirable. She began wishing she was a child again, so she wouldn't have to deal with life. Before long she fell into a pattern of partying every night, staying out until dawn, then going to work late, a hangover dulling her senses. Her work began to suffer and she was counseled by her supervisor. Maryanne hated confrontation. Afraid she would lose face, she said nothing, continuing to stuff her hurt feelings down with the rest of her pain.

Caught in a downward spiral, Maryanne's stress and anxiety were building up fast. In a matter of a few months, she went from a sunny, bright, attractive young woman at the top of her field to a morose, unkempt drunk, who showed up for work reeking of the previous night's partying. Finally, when her supervisor pointed out her latest mistake, Maryanne's defenses of denial and avoidance failed her. Her anger and pain broke through and she turned on the supervisor, shouting at her in coarse language, "F....you! It's not my fault!" Not surprisingly, Maryanne was given the choice of getting some help in counseling or a twelve-step program or lose her job on the spot. Maryanne's handwriting appears below.

At some point, pain needs to be faced. The longer we put off confronting it, the more difficult it becomes to manage successfully.

Defenses are important and useful only when used properly. A defense is like an antihistamine. When you have an allergy attack, you may take a pill to relieve the sneezing, itchy eyes and runny nose so you can live more comfortably. If you overuse the drug it loses its effectiveness and can even have a paradoxical result. In the same way, defense mechanisms can provide temporary relief from anxiety, but are only beneficial until a more realistic way of solving the problem can be found. A person who keeps depending upon his defenses may never learn more realistic ways of coping.

One or two aspirin is good for a mild headache, but a whole bottle could kill you. Emotional distress that requires continual monitoring and regulating cannot be cured with the "aspirin" of psychic defenses but needs direct attention. If you had a brain tumor, taking aspirin would not be of much use. You would probably seek a competent brain surgeon and get the help you needed. Likewise, long--term emotional distress should be addressed by a qualified psychological counselor. As a graphologist you can help that counselor by identifying the client's defense mechanisms in advance and providing a reasonable treatment plan for therapy.

The Dysfunctional Family

When a family is dysfunctional, the children generally do not notice that anything is "different" until they become adults, so they tend to grow up with a distorted view of family life. They think it is normal for a father to beat his wife and children; or for a mother to nag and scream at the family if she sees a spot of dirt-—and she is always seeing spots everywhere.

Psychiatrist Dr. Virginia Satir believes that 95% of families in the United States are dysfunctional; so, it follows that the overuse of defense mechanisms-—and the inability to recognize such overuse-—is incredibly common today.

What constitutes dysfunctional behavior in a family? A multitude of unhealthy habits, including alcoholism, drug addiction, religious fanaticism, and incest.

All dysfunctional families have in common the following characteristics:

> *Inconsistency in the way love was shown*
> *Constant criticism*
> *Behavior ranging on a broad spectrum from slightly odd to extremely bizarre*

According to writer Barbara Block, people who grow up in dysfunctional homes share several traits. The chart on the following page outlines these traits and some handwriting characteristics that demonstrate them.

NOTE: Please always keep in mind that when analyzing handwriting no individual characteristic means anything by itself but is only meaningful as it fits into the whole picture of the writing under consideration.

We will begin to examine some defenses and their equivalents in handwriting. The person who lives behind the wall of a defense system uses more than one defense; therefore, in the handwriting samples you will undoubtedly see crossovers and combinations of the various factors.

THIRTEEN DEFENSE MECHANISMS

1. Control

The person who chooses control as a defense must be in command of all interactions, feelings and behavior, at all times. His fear is that if he lets down his guard, he will lose control and be completely taken over. Aggressiveness is a side-effect of this defense. The aggressive person avoids being manipulated. The sample handwriting below is Freud.

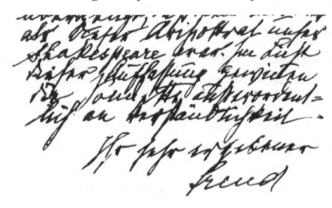

- ➤ *Persona Writing*
- ➤ *Retracing*
- ➤ *Narrowness in all zones*
- ➤ *Tension/Rigidity-low release*

2. Perfectionism

This person must be right in everything. A mental ruler is always being held up and no one, including himself, ever measures up. Fear and avoidance of the negative is the central organizing principle in his life, resulting in procrastination. If he doesn't finish a project, he can't be criticized for doing it wrong.

- ➤ *Overcontrol*
- ➤ *t bars*
- ➤ *i dots to left*
- ➤ *Tall upper zone*
- ➤ *Persona Writing*
- ➤ *Wide d, t loops*
- ➤ *Tall capitals*

We should, at all times, try to raise the price of our ink in almost all cases. Please review your special price lists and re-submit them (with mark-ups) to Don Cline for his approval.

3. Blame and excuses

The blaming person may censure himself or others, using this defense when control breaks down. He talks his way out of everything, manipulating words to his own end.

- ➢ *Sharp t bars and tics*
- ➢ *Thread writing*
- ➢ *Ending strokes turn back*
- ➢ *Complicated ovals Spoon c or c*
- ➢ *Odd formations in ovals*

4. Repression

A highly damaging defense, the person who uses repression doesn't talk. He never fully expresses any feeling, need or want. The feelings may be locked up to tightly that even though he may want to express himself, it is virtually impossible for him to get the words out.

> *Narrowness or Retracing*
> *Covering strokes*
> *Complicated ovals*
> *Extreme upper zone height*

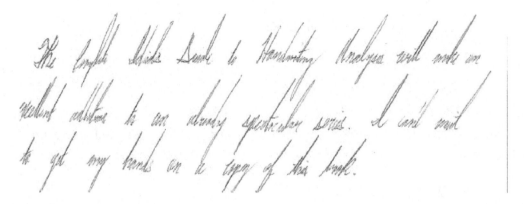

5. Denial and pretending

"We don't make mistakes" is the motto of people in denial. Mistakes reveal the flawed inner self and must be covered over. Alcoholics are famous for using this defense—"I can quit any time I want to…"

> *Single, double or triple-looped ovals*
> *Thread*
> *Cut off lower zone*
> *Thin upper zone*

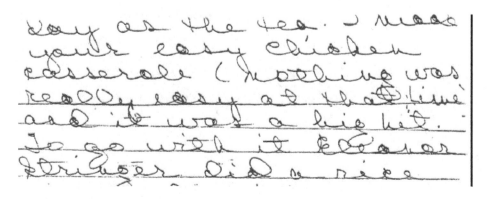

6. Unreliability

Interestingly, unreliability in relationships can be a sign that the person has been deeply disappointed. They have learned that if you don't trust anyone you won't be disappointed.

By making the other person angry with them through unreliable behavior, they don't have to get close. As a secondary gain, they prevent demands from being placed on them. Control is also a factor. When you keep someone waiting, for instance, as unreliable people often do, then you are controlling the other person's feelings.

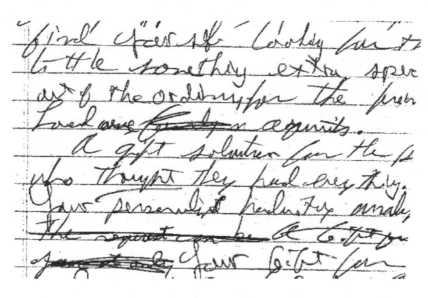

- ➢ *Stunted lower zone*
- ➢ *Long ending strokes*
- ➢ *Wide spacing between letters and words*
- ➢ *Wavy baseline*
- ➢ *Variable pressure*

7. Intellectualizing

Thinking your way out of a problem, making an objective appraisal and choosing the most rational means of resolving the conflict, or becoming absorbed in intellectual busywork helps one avoid dealing with the problem. This may be seen in a person who can coolly discuss his mother's death last week as if he were talking about a stranger. The feelings are pushed down, so they are only expressed through the intellect, rather than being felt through the emotions. One who constantly does crossword or other puzzles, reads a dozen newspapers a day and otherwise involving himself in intellectual pursuits keeps his mind too occupied to have to confront the unpleasant situation directly.

> ➤ *Too-tall upper zone*
> ➤ *Over-simplification*
> ➤ *Cut off lower zone*
> ➤ *Upper zone elaboration*
> ➤ *Small middle zone*

8. Idealization

One who can't accept that authority figures are imperfect may put them on a pedestal. It is likely that the father was missing in childhood. By idealizing an authority figure, he can avoid facing his doubts about his own self-worth.

> ➤ *Overly tall capitals,*
> ➤ *PPI with a disproportionate middle zone*
> ➤ *Elaborate capitals*

9. Dissociation

When the pain is too intense to bear, the person splits off parts of himself. This is what happens in cases of multiple personality (not to be confused with schizophrenia, which is a psychosis). Dissociative Identity Disorder (formerly known as Multiple Personality Disorder) is a result of extreme abuse, usually sexual, before the age of five. It is simply too painful to be that person any longer, so new personalities are created to deal with the pain. Dissociation may also occur with less dramatic intensity, such as when one "fades out" of his present reality for brief moments of time and indulges in fantasies.

> ➢ Extreme simplification to the point of skeletal writing.
> ➢ Extremely wide spacing overall, esp. between words and letters
> ➢ Printing adds to the above.

Indecision

When one feels helpless, confused, a victim, he may get others to tell him what to do and how to solve his personal problems. In that way, he denies responsibility for the results. Because others cannot solve someone else's personality problems, this "proves" there is no solution for his poor ego. By acting as a victim, he also avoids being taken advantage of.

- ➢ *Fluctuating slant, baseline, spacing*
- ➢ *Secondary thread writing*
- ➢ *End strokes fade out*
- ➢ *Small or weak PPI*

10.   Jealousy

The person who has problems with jealousy feels unlovable and insecure. His mother may not have felt close to the child, leaving him scared and angry, powerless to get love on his own merits. He is compelled to "prove" that no one loves him and his behavior is actually designed to force others to leave him. He demands all the attention by acting jealous. His attempt to make others responsible for his feelings sets him up for rejection because his demands are unreasonable.

- ➢ *Small, cramped lower zone*
- ➢ *Small or weak PPI*
- ➢ *Heavy pressure,*
- ➢ *Strong right slant*
- ➢ *Elaborate capitals*
- ➢ *Cramped initial loops on capitals*
- ➢ *Long t-bars at top or above the stem*
- ➢ *Finals that return and point back to the middle zone*

11.   Capitulation

The person who acquiesces all the time suffers from a fear of rejection. By giving in, he hopes to gain your approval. He wants appreciation and acceptance to bolster his sense of self, but even when the approval is given, can't accept it and feels worthless. The fear that he is being selfish if he puts his feelings first makes him deny his needs in favor of others.

Some one who I am physically attracted to, who's got a great personality, well built, and enjoy the same outdoor sport'l do. Romantic, a gentleman, loyal, non and good hearted & well treat

- ➤ *Rounded writing, esp. in the middle zone*
- ➤ *Many garlands*
- ➤ *"Pretty" or elaborate writing*
- ➤ *Hooked finals*

12.   Sensitiveness

Fear of criticism, of being seen as inadequate prompts this indiv idual to act inadequate which, in turn, provokes criticism. When his feelings are hurt by perceived criticism, he can make others feel bad by making them responsible for his feelings and condemning them. Likely, he grew up in a critical atmosphere where faultfinding was a way of life. He learned that he could never be adequate and heard selectively, only the negative things penetrated. His self-criticism is far worse than anything another person could heap on him.

I am happy to be : today at the San Ber Mountain arts and crafts. My handwriting will res I really am inside.

> ➤ *Wide loops in upper zone*
> ➤ *Angled PPI*
> ➤ *Above-average right slant*
> ➤ *Left pointed angles at the baseline*
> ➤ *Narrow e's*

Developing Active Coping Skills

There are positive ways of dealing with stress and pain in our lives. Learning to take responsibility for one's actions is the first step. By accepting everything that we think or say or do as our own choices and recognizing that whatever has happened in our lives—good or bad—is the result of those choices, we discover that we can also change what happens to us in the future. Sometimes changes in the environment are called for; often there is simply a need to change our responses to the environment.

Recognizing the need for change is a major stride in the process of growth. Making those changes, either alone or with the help of a trained counselor, perhaps even along with graphotherapy (handwriting exercises to change personality), puts one firmly on the path to increased potential for happiness.

The foregoing is a very large subject that cannot hope to be fully addressed in a brief monograph. However, this overview will provide a glimpse at the possibilities.

Personality characteristics of adults from dysfunctional homes

> ✓ *Difficulty saying no*
> ✓ *Not sure how they feel about anything*
> ✓ *Judge themselves without mercy*
> ✓ *Lie unnecessarily——say what they think they should*
> ✓ *Take themselves too seriously (can't have fun)*
> ✓ *Difficulty with relationships*
> ✓ *Can't discern appropriateness in behavior*
> ✓ *Impulsive, hasty decisions*
> ✓ *Procrastinate—can't finish without pressure*
> ✓ *Feel different from others, cover up*
> ✓ *Will do anything for approval*
> ✓ *Either super-responsible or super-irresponsible*
> ✓ *Problems trusting others or sharing responsibility*
> ✓ *Extremely loyal, even when undeserved*
> ✓ *Depressed, due to sense of inadequacy (can lead to substance abuse)*
> ✓ *Difficulty making changes, may self-sabotage*

Handwriting Characteristics

- ➢ dished t bars, variable baseline
- ➢ variable slant, pressure, baseline
- ➢ downstrokes stab back at baseline
- ➢ complicated ovals, too tall upper zone
- ➢ copybook or persona writing; rigidity
- ➢ unfinished lower zone; abrupt disconnections
- ➢ jump--up letters; capitals in inappropriate places
- ➢ too fast; illegible
- ➢ missing t--bars & i dots, letters don't return to baseline
- ➢ retracing, covering strokes, persona
- ➢ too rounded; dished t bars
- ➢ copybook, small; or large, irregular
- ➢ abrupt breaks; short terminal strokes; wide spaces between words
- ➢ rounded; high regularity; copybook
- ➢ light pressure; downward baseline; small writing; small PPI
- ➢ rigidity

This page intentionally left blank

Beneath it All: the lower zone and the subconscious

By Sheila Lowe, MS, CG, CFDE

© 1984 by Sheila R. Lowe
Revised 1998
All rights reserved. No portion of this book may be reproduced,
by any process or technique, without the express written
consent of the author, except small excerpts, for purpose of review.

Beneath It All:

The Lower Zone and the Subconscious

Keeper of secrets, gateway to the unconscious,
the lower zone holds the mysteries of the psyche.

As long as we are alive we use energy. We use it to perform the work of the personality, discharging it into various areas of life—thinking, feeling, and acting.

Like mass, energy can be transformed for different uses and, though limited in supply, is indestructible. Thus, if energy migrates from one part of a system, it must appear in another. Think of it like a sausage-shaped balloon filled with air. If you squeeze the balloon one third from the end the air will flow into the other two-thirds. The amount of air in the balloon has not changed but is distributed differently.

Perhaps you expend the bulk of your energy in physical activities, de-emphasizing mental processes. Or, you apply your energy to thinking and planning at the expense of physical performance. Like the balloon, the same amount of air (energy) is available, but it is reshaped for use according to your needs of the moment. When you are at rest your energy is used for breathing and maintaining life support. It may also be used to repress unpleasant or dangerous impulses.

Behavior manifests, to a large degree, in how energy is distributed throughout the personality. As an expressive behavior, a handwriting sample clearly indicates how energy is distributed and where the writer chooses to focus it. Whether he spends most of his time thinking, feeling, or acting, or balances energy throughout, his handwriting will reveal it.

The Three Parts of Personality

Man seems to have a propensity for dividing many parts of life into threes. In the pantheon of deities there are many triune gods or trinities. Religion speaks of heaven, earth and hell. Psychologists name the thinking, feeling and acting parts of personality. In all humanity we refer to spirit, mind and body.

There may still be arguments over some of his theories, but Sigmund Freud, father of modern psychology, applied this triune paradigm when he identified three parts of personality: the id, ego and superego—individual elements but never really separate. Although each element has its own particular functions, they continually link and interact with each other.

In handwriting we can see the actions of the id, ego, and superego in their various parts. All act upon each other, not always in harmony, and though we may make broad generalizations about them, no real analysis can be made without considering how the parts fit into the whole.

Put another way, no discussion of a single element of handwriting, or a single element of personality can be complete without taking into consideration the whole. Therefore, while this paper's main focus is the id and how its energy manifests in handwriting, it would be a ridiculous oversimplification to leave the other aspects of personality unmentioned.

"Id Writing"

The id is the earliest aspect of personality to appear. Its sole purpose is to obtain pleasure by reducing tension caused by common biological urges such as the need and desire for food, sex, material possessions, safety and love. These innate urges nudge the baby (and later the adult) to satisfy them by making him uncomfortable. In other words, tension is produced when these needs and desires go unsatisfied.

The id either discharges its energy into gratifying those urges or "binding" the energy for future use.

The id knows only that it wants something (tension is produced) and its energy is directed into obtaining the object of its desire. A personality ruled by the id never matures past the infantile stage. Just as a baby has no interest in delaying gratification, the id-directed adult is impatient, easily frustrated and restless until he gets what he wants, regardless of whether or not his desire is appropriate.

A purely id handwriting is one where energy dissipates without a specific focus. We have all seen the person who can't sit still, whose toes are always tapping, who fidgets constantly until he gets what he wants. This type of person suffers from an infantile inability to delay gratification. An infant does not care if its desires are appropriate to the moment or not and, like an infant, the id is demanding, impulsive, irrational and pleasure-seeking.

All humans have "id impulses," but not everyone acts on every impulse the moment it is experienced. Imagine being in the grocery store. You've just finished shopping when you meander past the bakery section. You feel a sudden tug in that direction as the chocolate eclairs seductively whisper your name. Yes, you're on a diet, but they look *so* delicious with fresh whipped cream oozing from the sides, satiny chocolate drizzling down onto the plate— it's just too much to expect you to resist. Impulsively, you call out to the counter help, "I'll take one!"

Your desire for the eclair was an id impulse, and like a pleasure-seeking infant, you were driven to satisfy that desire.

In handwriting, the id energy manifests in poorly controlled or uncontrolled movement. Like the sample above, there will be a great deal of variability in size, slant, baseline, etc. Id energy is easy to see in the lower zone lower, which is the area below the baseline (printed or imaginary line of writing), the loops on g,y,p,f,j,q. This area represents the subconscious and unconscious. When the lower zone is emphasized in some special way, such as extra length or width on those loops, the writer needs instant gratification or he experiences continued tension.

Fantasy or Imagination?

For the id, the dream is as good as the reality and does not differentiate between them; one is as good as the other. We dream about what we want. In handwriting, the lower zone is where we go to dream or fantasize. Just thinking about something won't make the dream come true, however. In order to make a dream into reality, it must be brought into the middle zone for realistic planning and execution. A medium length/width lower zone which returns to the baseline is the ideal for this purpose. In a copybook writing, medium length is 1.5-2.0 times the height of the middle zone. Medium width is .5-1.0.

An overinflated lower zone suggests inability to reduce the tension produced by the dream or desire. The energy is simply floating around in the subconscious, lazily enjoying the fantasy, but failing to bring it into the middle zone (the area of reality and ego) to make it real. The unfortunate consequence often is that all the energy is spent on the dream, not leaving enough for the practical application.

Some newer graphologists tend to confuse fantasy with imagination. The main difference is that imagination is a conscious, upper zone activity. Fantasy, on the other hand, is a lower zone activity because it is unconscious.

Unproductive Fantasy

A moderately (not an extremely) inflated upper zone loop (upper loops on the letters b, h, l, k) represents active imagination, which can help turn the dream into a reality. Upper zone imagination never mistakes fantasy for reality, but it provides the mental impetus needed to obtain or create the object of the dream or fantasy.

The lower zone (id) can only wish or act, it does not think. Thinking, planning, and reasoning is the work of the ego or middle zone (vowels and lowercase letters that have no upper or lower extensions, or parts of letters that exist above the baseline, but not the upper loops) and the superego (upper zone).

The Ego

At this point, we need to know a little bit about where the other parts of personality fit in.

As the infant grows into a young child, he begins learning to manage his impulses and control them until the right time and place to discharge them. Managing impulses is the function of the ego. Words such as "learning," "perceiving," "remembering," "discriminating," and "reasoning" are associated with the ego.

In a healthy personality, the ego behaves as the governor of all the parts. It works on the reality principle, which postpones the satisfaction of desires until the proper time. Put a plastic bunny in a baby's hand and the bunny will immediately go into the baby's mouth. When the baby is hungry, it tries to eat whatever is at hand. With growth and maturity, he learns to postpone eating until something edible is presented. In other words, while the id provides the energy for the wish, the ego tells the personality to plan realistically for gratification and controls its acting on the wish.

vention speakers and ordering infor mation

In a well-balanced handwriting, the zones interact harmoniously. The writer has cultivated an ability to plan and act in a reasonable manner, controlling his impulses as appropriate, and satisfying them at the proper time.

Blocked Energy

Energy sometimes becomes blocked. This can happen in a number of ways. For instance, the ego may signal to the id that its desires are inappropriate and attempt to intercept them.

When the desires are stronger than the ego's defenses, the id overwhelms the ego and does what it wants. The result is impulsive behavior, such as in the chocolate eclair example. When a normally calm and controlled person loses his temper, it is a sign that the id energy has broken through the ego's defenses.

Conflict is produced when the ego or superego works to block the discharge of energy from the id. The id energy attempts to break through, either into action or fantasy. Remember, *the id does not think; it simply wishes or acts.* For the id, "the wish is as good as the act."

Energy cannot be destroyed, so blocked energy must be displaced or transformed. That is, it may be sublimated or channeled into some substitute activity.

Imagine, for example, that your lover is away on a trip and your emotional and sexual needs are not fully satisfied. You may release the tension brought on by your lower zone instinctual urges by substituting another object for what you really want—your lover. You might do this by looking at photos of the two of you together, by talking about him to a friend, or by (sublimating) putting that energy into cleaning the house, playing tennis or throwing yourself into work, etc.

Reversed pressure in the lower zone can be a result of blocked energy. It demonstrates a re-channeling of energy into a substitute pursuit (see "compensation").

The Superego

How often has your ego told you that something you wanted wasn't good for you, but you did it anyway? Did you punish yourself by becoming anxious, having an accident, acting confused and out of touch with reality, or making awful faux pas in speaking or writing? If you did, that was the superego part of your personality making its presence felt.

The superego is your "internal parent" or your conscience. It looks over your shoulder, reminding you of what you should or should not do. Maybe you would like to throttle your child who is having a tantrum, but the superego controls the dangerous impulse and keeps you out of jail. You work hard all year and give yourself a vacation in Hawaii, because the superego is providing a reward. You ate that chocolate eclair and your superego punished you with an upset stomach. The superego sees things as they should be rather than as they actually are. It is otherwise known as your conscience, or parent part of the personality. The ego is the adult member of the triad and the id is the child.

From time to time, we make slips of the tongue, known as a Freudian Slip (the formal term is "parapraxis"). Some feeling or behavior that you were attempting to repress comes out unexpectedly in speech. Such slips may reveal deeper thoughts and are due to unconscious motivations.

Following are some common examples:

1. Let's be the *breast* of friends.
2. An appointment is scheduled for Tuesday. You accidentally say, "okay, I'll be there Wednesday." Could this mean you wish the appointment were on Wednesday or that you would like to miss it altogether?
3. Reading it wrong: A man is reading a personals ad. The woman actually wrote "I like men with lots of hair." He reads it as, "I like men who've lost their hair." the man is bald.
4. A man writes to his girlfriend, wish you were her (here).
5. Man "accidentally" calls his wife "Mom."

"A Freudian slip is when you mean one thing, but you say your mother."

If you make a slip of the tongue or grossly misinterpret something, ask yourself if there might be something deeper to it. Or, maybe this time, a cigar is just a cigar.

We have looked at an "id handwriting," where there is too much release, too much variability. At the other end of the spectrum is the personality with a very strong *superego*, which tends to be uptight much of the time because the energy is largely directed into controlling the id.

The strong superego manifests in handwriting as the overcontrol that results in rigid and narrow forms or retracing of letters. The writing is overall contracted and lacking in release movement. Generally, the person whose superego controls them has come from a background of very strict parenting.

In summary:

> ➢ *The id says I WANT IT NOW!*
> ➢ *The ego says WAIT FOR THE APPROPRIATE TIME*
> ➢ *The superego says NO, YOU CANNOT HAVE IT!*

If the id is in control, the writer will be hedonistic. If the superego is in control he will be moralistic. If the ego is in control, the behavior is more realistic.

Conscious/Unconscious

Id energy exists on an unconscious, instinctual level. Yet, it constantly makes itself felt consciously in daily life. Freud's psychoanalytic theories claimed that the id energy, which drives the person, is made up entirely of sexual and aggressive drives (which has been strongly disputed). He believed that to discover all the experiences hidden in the unconscious would mean to understand the reasons for an individual's behavior.

Freud view the greater part of the personality as being submerged in the unconscious like an iceberg, with only the tip sticking out above the water. It was his opinion that humans repress most memories as being too painful to deal with.

It's true that most memories are too weak or too unimportant to remember. Nevertheless, all memories are stored in some brain cell for later retrieval. Thus, when you need a particular memory and are ready to receive it, it will surface, only to disappear once again when the need for it has passed.

Dealing with some of the material in the subconscious is extremely important for happiness and emotional growth. Dealing with painful memories makes more energy is available to work constructively on relationships and other life situations.

Compensation

We have touched briefly on sublimation and substitution; now we consider compensation.

To compensate means to make up for a loss. Consider the person who, though he feels quite timid inside, comes on strong. He *over*compensates for insecurity by his aggressive behavior. Another person might overeat or drink too much to compensate for feeling unloved.

A normal pressure pattern in right-handed writing is produced by a rhythmic balance of contraction and release movement when propelling the writing instrument across the paper. This requires slightly lighter pressure on upstrokes than downstrokes. One form of compensation that may be identified in handwriting is displaced pressure, where the force is exerted against the pen and/or paper opposite to the normal manner.

Note: displaced pressure is commonly seen in the handwriting of left-handers and while the interpretation is the same, it is given less significance.

Displaced pressure reveals an upset between the contraction and release pattern, which interferes with the body/mind/emotions rhythm. In the writing of a person who is compensating for some deficit, either real or imagined, you might see light downstrokes and heavy upstrokes, or pressure on horizontal strokes, as in extra heavy t-crosses.

It is difficult to see in a copy, but the arrows in the sample show displaced pressure in the lower zone, where the pressure is heavier on the upstroke, rather than the downstroke.

In normal pressure patterns, the downstroke characterizes movement toward a goal, which requires somewhat greater exertion or heavier pressure. Once the goal is achieved and the (id) energy is released, the pressure lightens. In reversed pressure, the heavier pressure is on the upstroke rather than the downstroke. The writer is misdirecting the energy and ends up holding back when he should be releasing his feelings and vice versa. The area of personality affected by the displacement depends upon the zone(s) in which the pressure is displaced.

Dr. David Mayer, in *Exploring Graphology,* Vol. 5, Num. 5, describes displaced pressure in the lower zone as a displacement of the physical and materialistic drives. He states,

> *"Displaced pressure indicates an insecure ego which seeks security through its disordered personality functioning. The personality sustains argument in seeking reassurance of his beliefs or opinions; he manipulates in order to satisfy his urge to win...[which] calls for many compensatory patterns of behavior."*

Handwriting and Instinct

The instinctual urges reside in the lower zone, where motives are prompted, not by conscious thought but rather by a biological imperative, the id impulses. As we have seen, the drive for food, physical activities, material possessions and sex, as well as productive energy, is regulated by this area of personality.

Lower zone needs are instinctive physical cravings that we do not have to think about consciously unless some trauma intervenes and brings the urge to our conscious focus. For instance, an eating disorder, sleep disorder or some form of substance abuse would propel the natural and normal drives out of the instinctual sphere and the lower zone activity becomes conscious and outwardly manifest by its results—malnutrition, insomnia, neurosis, alcoholism, addiction, etc.

Not all unconscious activities are instinctive but all instinctive activities come from the unconscious. Sometimes the two will cross. Carl Jung offers the example of a person taking a walk who suddenly comes face to face with a poisonous snake. Naturally, he recoils in a violent fright; this is a normal instinct. However, if he habitually experiences the same feelings when he sees a chicken, he is suffering from a phobia of unconscious origin based on past experience, and not of natural instinct.

Intuition

Intuition is an instinctive, unconscious process not produced by any given stimuli. It may be defined as 'knowing what you know without knowing how you know it.' Intuition begins as an unconscious process in the lower zone. When the intuitive perception is ready to surface in conscious thought the writer may break open a space in the writing line, mid-word, to allow knowledge room to sprout. See the arrows in the following sample.

Intuition is part of the individual's genetic makeup, an instinctive perception of truth without a rational consideration of the facts. Intuition originates in the lower zone. One knows intuition is present when it erupts into the conscious, as seen by sudden smooth breaks (air strokes) along the baseline of writing. Some call them "intuitive breaks." It is

important to note, however, that to be intuitive, the break should be smooth, not abrupt or choppy; otherwise, it is more likely a jumping to conclusions, which may be way off base, rather than true intuition.

It is noteworthy that many highly intuitive people, including some psychics, write with no breaks in words at all. This suggests that they are getting their information from a source other than the instincts of the lower zone. In such cases, the often writing has a flat, open quality, is thready with some neglect of form, which similarly allows them to be open to the environment, but in a different way than with those who rely on "hunches."

The Lower Zone and Repression

Besides being the repository of the id, the lower zone also symbolizes the writer's attitudes about the past and the need for security and mothering. Therefore, sentiments toward the mother show up in this zone, as does the writer's ability to leave the past behind and use his experiences constructively.

The lower zone area—the subconscious and unconscious—holds all lost memories, including thoughts that are too weak or too unimportant to rise to the surface. Those repressed memories and feelings that are too painful to think about hide deep in the unconscious yet are revealed in a page of writing.

In his book, *Handwriting: A Personality Projection,* Frank Victor speaks of the lower zone as being below, or the ground, "the basis of life, the source of food and security." He described "soil" and "dirt" as unclean things, historically closely connected with fertility and thereby base, something to hide.

Everyone has secrets of one kind or another, things they might be ashamed to have others know about them, or secret wishes and desires. There are some experiences that are so unbearable, we prefer to keep them hidden. When one deliberately or subconsciously pushes away uncomfortable or unpleasant thoughts, it is called repression.

Some people might think that the copybook sample below is attractive because it is so regular. However, to a handwriting analyst it shows a strongly repressed personality. There is too little release in the machine-like progression across the page. It is written exactly as it was taught in school with no room for change that results in emotional growth.

With every dip of the pen below the baseline the lower zone reveals what the writer works so hard to hide. The pen recreates the situations we would rather avoid; a perpetual reliving of the events that first provoked the repression.

Four score and seven years ago ou fathers brought forth upon this cc tinent a new nation, conceived in liberty, and dedicated to the prop that all men are created equal.

The lower zone encompasses the entire area of writing below the baseline. Lower zone loops appear on the letters g,y,p,f, and z, but also, parts of other letters which fall below the baseline where they don't belong become significant parts of the lower zone by their very inappropriate appearance there.

A well-formed lower zone indicates the healthy satisfaction of physical pleasures. As mentioned earlier, copybook or school-type writing demands that lower zone length be one and one-half time the middle zone height. The width of the loop should equal ½ the middle zone height/width. For example, if the middle zone is copybook, measuring 3mm, a copybook lower zone will be 4.5mm long and 1.5mm wide.

In many handwritings the length, width, and/or shape of the lower zone is far different from the prescribed model. As always, we must examine the entire writing to understand what is taking place in the writer's subconscious.

Although no element of handwriting should be considered outside the context of the sample in which it appears, for the sake of analysis, some graphologists endow certain letters with particular significance. It is vital that the analyst corroborate any findings on a single sign with other evidence in the writing before making a conclusion. No one indicator means anything by itself.

Some claim the letter "y" especially relates to the writer's attitudes toward money, that the "g" is sexually significant and that "p" is oriented toward physical matters. Interestingly, there are different interpretations about the letter "f," which some graphologists claim represents views toward family.

For example, it is thought that if the lower loop on an "f" is pointed at the bottom, it may signify hostility toward the writer's family. A large knot on the lower "f" loop denotes family pride. Others relate a large lower loop on the "f" to an excessive desire for food. An extra-long lower loop may be found in those with an interest in researching their family history.

Lower zone length reveals the strength of the writer's drive for material and physical pursuits. The longer the loop, the greater the drive. With some inflation in the loop (not overly exaggerated), the drive can be channeled into productive activity.

When the pressure fades out on the upstroke before reaching the baseline, the writer may not have much stamina for lower zone activities. The energy fades with the flow of ink. This may be the person who falls asleep halfway through lovemaking after a passionate start and may signify either the repression of very deep hostility or, possibly, a physical problem. Or it might just be a young mother trying to distribute her energy in too many directions. Context is everything.

In the sample below, note how the bottoms of the loops fades out, then picks up again to complete the loop. This person's energy fades, but she will get a second wind.

Sex as tranquilizer?

A long lower zone with moderate fullness generally indicates a productive, active person who includes other people in his activities. An extremely long lower zone, however, as shown below, where the lower zone is three or more times as long as the middle zone height, reveals restlessness and compulsive activity—a need to be doing, experiencing, feeling, all the time. This type of writer may choose to use sex as a tranquilizer to quell an underlying anxiety rather than as a release of loving feelings toward his partner. He may feel the need to engage in sexual activity several times a day to keep his anxiety under control.

The handwriting analyst must determine whether the lower zone width supports the

extreme length to allow for productive activity, or whether it is an aimless discharge of energy. A very short lower zone shows limited interest or de-emphasis on the physical.

Jung stated that there needs to be a continual going back and forth between past experiences, present activities and future plans. Writing rhythm and movement plus zonal distribution reveals how balanced these back-and-forth motions are.

Lower Zone Distortions

The ideal lower loop begins at the baseline and moves downward, with a rounded bottom and an upstroke that crosses the downstroke, ending back at the baseline. The baseline of writing is the line of demarcation between reality and fantasy.

The writer's ability to plunge into his past and bring his experiences up into reality to use in his daily life is seen in the way he treats the plunge into the lower zone and the return to the surface at the baseline.

Distortions in the shape of the lower loop or turning in the wrong direction or are a red flag. For example, angular lower zone formations manifest hidden aggression and hostility.

Because this area represents the past, all the way back to the beginning of life, angles in the lower zone often signify hostility toward mother and, by extension, all women, especially if the angles are pointing leftward (toward the past).

President Bill Clinton's handwriting below contains soft angles in the lower zone, which literally softens the hidden aggression. They do not point to the past, but pull right, to the future and male authority figures. This makes sense because he is said to have had a good relationship with his mother, but his father was missing.

When the lower loops form an acute triangle, we find suppressed aggression. The triangle stores an enormous amount of energy which is likely acted out in intensely critical behavior toward a mate. The following is an extreme example.

Angles with a slight tick are more a sign of impatience, bad temper and irritability. The sharp i-dots add to the irritability in the sample below.

When a cradle-like garland formation appears in the lower zone, ending with a leftward stroke, it implies a strong need for mothering and security. The movement is toward the past and the beginning of life, where mother was (supposed to be) the nurturer. By leaving the lower zone stroke hanging and pointed to the left side of the paper, the writer sets himself up for disappointment. His emotional needs cannot be fulfilled because he is continually searches for someone to take care of him, and it is impossible to go back and change the past.

The following is an example of the cradle form.

I love to hike, read, enjoy environment. Naps are a you enjoy the writing.

Here is another example of the cradle in a too-rounded writing.

the following steps will be taken to re: issues discussed at today's meeting.

Men who adopt this lower zone form (less common) may appear very strong and self-confident in their professional lives, yet at home they want their wives and lovers to baby and coddle them.

Sometimes the cradle formation ends with a sharp, thinned-out stroke. If other signs of aggression are also present (e.g.: club strokes, angles, sharp t-bars, rigidity), the writer may strike out at his partner, demanding caretaking from him/her (though this seems to be largely a male phenomenon) in a cruel, even brutal, manner.

I knew that this is a true of my handwriting Kathy and I to Europe in the spring.

Another form of leftward lower zone is a completed loop which pulls so strongly to the left that it lies on its side. This form is often adopted by homosexual men who feel a strong pull to the past and have formed an unbreakable bond with their mothers. There is also a need to avoid their fathers or other men (symbolism of males and authority figures in handwriting is movement towards the right side of the paper). At best, it is a sign of a poorly developed sexual identity.

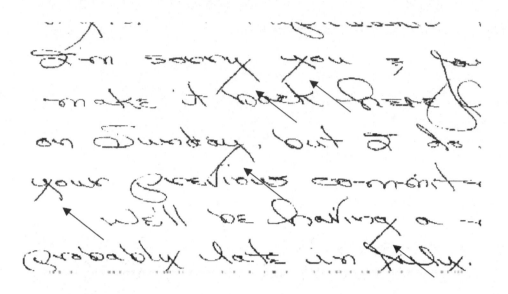

On the opposite side of the coin is the lower loop that pulls to the right, signifying rebellion against the mother and rejection of what she symbolizes; but also pushing against the father and male authority figures. In the sample below, note that the "h" which does not belong in the lower zone, is there inappropriately and also pulls to the right. This suggests that the writer is poking around in the past, trying to figure out "what happened?"

In some cases, the bottom of the lower zone seems to "drop out," leaving a formation resembling the letter x. This phenomenon is created by an airstroke. In other words, at some point in the downstroke, there is a subtle lift of the pen, which is replaced on the paper somewhere during the upstroke, thereby leaving a blank space in the lower zone letter.

The analyst needs to determine whether the bottom is falling out of one particular letter or all lower zone letters. Often, the cause is physiological, rather than (or in addition to) an emotional loss. It would be wise to ask whether the writer suffered an injury to the legs or feet, or some other medical reason that might be reflected in the handwriting. Handwriting analysts are not psychic, sometimes we need additional information in order to make the most accurate analysis.

If this is not the case then the analyst can conclude that a painful situation is interfering with the writer's ability to move forward in his/her life. Because the lower zone represents the writer's past and his roots, the gap in the lower zone expresses a desire to avoid going back and looking at where she came from, or it may be related to a specific, painful incident, such as a broken love relationship.

Fantasy can enrich an individual's life if not overindulged. However, a person who becomes a Walter Mitty who lives in his fantasies most of the time, may be on the road to psychosis. Extremely wide lower loops show that the writer is spending so much time fantasizing about what he hopes to accomplish that he wastes his productive energy, leaving little to get done what he dreams about.

This type of inflated loop is found in the writings of people who flirt a great deal, bragging about their sexual prowess. However, when it comes down to the nitty gritty, the men are often impotent and the women sexually inhibited.

Extremely narrow lower loops signify repression of the biological urges. The writer leaves no room for fantasy that could enrich his life. Guilt and fear of intimacy inhibit the normal

release of his deep feelings into sexual activity. The squeezing of lower loops suggests great anxiety, which might be expressed through physical symptoms, such as headaches and backaches.

One who represses large parts of himself becomes stilted and lifeless. His ability to act spontaneously and be creative are stifled because he is constantly censoring his impulses and feelings. The superego exercises strict control over the id impulses. Along with the squeezed loops, the writing below has a very tight rhythm.

The writer of the following sample was raped at the age of 14. In adult life she barters sexual favors with her husband in exchange for expensive materials goods. Theirs is a marriage of convenience and she has lovers on the side whom she lures into relationships and then drops when they are "hooked." Note the angle in the lower zone, which is also twisted, revealing the strength of her hostility.

Occasionally, we see a middle zone circle with a tiny downstroke and a completely disconnected loop superimposed over the downstroke, or there may be two disconnected circles. Unless the analyst uses a magnifier, he may not realize there is a separation between the two parts of the letter.

In either case, the writer has completely isolated (disconnected) himself from his sexual appetites, which are too uncomfortable for him to face; or he may come from a harsh religious background where it was considered a sin to have sexual passions and he had to cut himself off from those passions. He denies that he owns any such feelings because to admit to them would make him feel unclean.

A highly unusual example of a disconnected loop is seen in the following sample, where the writer, a woman in her 50's, superimposes a form that resembles a capital G over the

80

downstroke of all her lower zone letters (except the f's). In fact, the letter G is part of her initials.

Some graphologists have commented that perhaps this woman is musical and the forms represent a treble clef. Such an interpretation may or may not be correct; however, such a strange form in the lower zone must have a far deeper association.

In fact, the writer's husband engages in exotic sexual practices in his office with his secretaries and with his wife's knowledge. One might speculate that for this woman to tolerate such behavior, sexual abuse is likely part of her background.

A form known as the "felon's claw" (a misnomer because it is not often seen in the handwriting of felons) is frequently found in the lower zones of the handwriting of (mostly) women who were sexually abused and feel guilty about it. The claw-shape is a holding down of the painful memories from the past, and also a holding onto them.

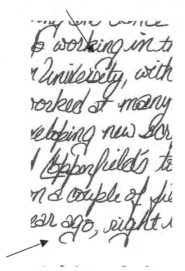

During an appearance on a Los Angeles radio program, representatives of the Prostitutes Anonymous organization presented the sad, if unsurprising, fact that without exception, every woman in the group of former and recovering sex workers had been abused, sexually or otherwise, as young children.

Whether or not sexual abuse is discernable in a handwriting depends upon the ability of the victim to work through her painful experiences and grow emotionally, leaving the old pain behind. When the abuse is unresolved there are likely to be unusual forms in the lower zone, such as the previous two shown here. There is a wide range of such forms and as always, they need to be considered and interpreted within the context of the handwriting in which they appear. (Sexual abuse is covered elsewhere in this collection of papers).

This sample contains angry hooks that remain in the lower zone and point to the left, which suggests the anger he feels at mother is taken out on women in general. Other signs of irritability, such as the downstroke that starts high above the "p" and the oddly wavy "t-bar," conflict with the garland middle zone. The writer's pain runs deep and he does his best to deny it and rationalize it away.

Those who are able to release their feelings will find that their handwriting reflects the emotional growth as unusual lower zone forms straighten out.

The simple, straight downstroke with no upstroke is a common form. It has less significance if the "stick form," as it is called, occurs only on the last letter of a word, as this plain downstroke adds to simplicity and speed, which is desirable. If, however, all lower zone letters are unfinished, the writer is cutting off his desires altogether.

This differs from repression because in the retraced loop, the person may secretly admit his desires but refuse to allow himself to satisfy them. When he cuts off the upstroke completely, he does not even admit that the desire is present. Sticklike forms in the lower zone, in combination with wide spaces between words and/or lines, indicate that the writer withdraws emotionally in sexual situations, creating distance from his significant other. He might do this by provoking an argument, constantly working late, hiding behind the newspaper, or being unfaithful. Anything to create some space will do. Once he reaches his comfort zone, he will begin seeking closeness again, thereby perpetuating a vicious cycle.

Fear of intimacy

A lower zone with many varied forms expresses the need for interesting or unusual sexual adventures. High form level writing with few negative signs might imply that he seeks such variety through healthy outlets. However, with low form level, muddy pressure, and bizarre formations it might be that the writer acts out sexually in a "kinky," perhaps even deviant, manner. This is often true of twisted structures in the lower zone.

Covering up past activities

Arcades in the lower zone symbolize a hiding of past events, possibly abuse of some type. The degree of repression in the writing gives a clue whether or not the writer is aware of what he is hiding. The following sample also reveals the writer's need to draw attention to herself in the strokes that come up and over the word.

Confusion of activities and lack of self-knowledge

Tangled loops in the lower zone that hang down and interfere with the line below reveal confusion between desires and actions, a lack of organization and self-knowledge. By attempting to cram so much into every day and night, such a writer may have a hard time keeping a schedule straight. She needs a good calendar, or someone to follow behind her and pick up the items that fall through the cracks.

Time Line Theory

The late Dr. William Hallow postulated the theory that the lower zone is like a time line. The time of birth is found at the lowest point of the loop and the present at the baseline (reality). He felt that the point where the upstroke crosses the downstroke, if it crosses in the lower zone rather than at the baseline, is the time in the writer's life when major trauma occurred.

So, if the writer is 40 years old and the upstroke crosses approximately halfway up the downstroke, he experienced trauma around age 20 which is yet unresolved. This most interesting theory has been tested and supported by many analysts.

Middle zone letters sometimes extend below the baseline, or lower zone letters cross at the baseline, with the final stroke dipping back down into the unconscious area. When this happens, the writer has suffered a major life disappointment and is searching in his subconscious for something, often, the nurturing or mothering that he missed. He continually goes back, looking for satisfaction, but it always eludes him because he doesn't work through the early childhood situation which caused the urge to return to that stage.

The lower zone offers a wealth of information and we have barely scratched the surface. It would require many volumes to adequately cover all the aspects of handwriting that need to be considered when drawing conclusions and making a synthesis. A good grasp of how lower zone energy is discharged provides a key that will help unlock the mysteries of the psyche.

Miscellaneous notes: lower zone related to sex

- Lower zone length = degree of drive
- Lower zone width = degree of satisfaction
- Unusual forms = the writer likely experienced sexual abuse
- Cradle LZ: uses sexuality to get affection and attention; confuses sexuality with love.
- Reverse pressure in LZ: lack of effective release, sublimation of drives.
- End stroke goes back into LZ = disappointment, looking for more.
- "Felon's claw" in LZ: fear or guilt related to sex, "sex is bad," "sex is dirty."
- Triangle LZ - in female = domineering; must be in control of the sex act Triangle LZ - in male = Madonna-prostitute syndrome; superiority, control; lack of release.
- Knots in LZ = sexual abuse experiences likely.
- LZ ends to left = out of touch with sexuality.
- LZ pulls to left = Return to mother.
- Lack of interzonal balance = unreliable in relationships
- Directional pressure from right (lower loop bends inward) = may "talk big" about sexual prowess, tell dirty jokes, etc., but fears sex.

Motivations and Handwriting
What Makes You Tick?

By Sheila R. Lowe, CG, MS, CFDE

Motivations and Handwriting–What Makes You Tick? Copyright © 2011 by Sheila Lowe, CG, MS

All rights reserved. No portion of this book may be reproduced, by any process or technique, without the express written consent of the author, except small excerpts, for purpose of review.

www.sheilalowe.com

Email: sheila@sheilalowe.com

Abraham Maslow and the Pyramid of Needs

According to humanistic psychologist Abraham Maslow, all humans are motivated by the same basic set of somethings. Early in his research, Maslow recognized that some of those basic needs are stronger and take precedence over others. He also found that unless the stronger needs are met first, the less urgent ones may be neglected.

The bottom level of the pyramid comprises the most basic physiological needs, followed by the need for safety and security, followed by the need for love and belonging, followed the need for esteem. At the top of the pyramid is a level that Maslow believed relatively few people ever attain. He called that level self-actualization.

As graphologists, it is vital for us to understand the basic psychology behind various theories of personality. Simply knowing what the various elements of handwriting "means" is not enough to provide a comprehensive analysis of a writer. A good grasp of personality development is an integral part of the graphologist's education. Our task in this case is to explore how the various needs levels identified by Maslow may be manifested in handwriting, which can help determine whether the writer is currently at one or more lower needs levels or has achieved self-actualization.

By identifying through our study of handwriting which needs are given the strongest priority, the graphologist is able to gain a clearer understanding of a writers' core personality—we open a window to the motivations behind the behavior laid down in ink on the page.

Thus, this paper will give an overview of the five levels of the Maslow pyramid in the context of how one's life experiences, both as children and as adults, may influence the ways in which one responds to his (or her) common set of basic needs. We will also meet through their handwriting and history some of the well-known individuals whom Maslow identified as self-actualized.

Before we begin, an important note: there is no "this means that" correlation between handwriting and personality traits. We can talk only in general terms about

what sorts of handwriting characteristics we might see in each needs level. There are thousands of variables in handwriting and the whole picture must always be kept in mind. Meanings change depending upon the particular constellation of elements that appear in the writing sample you are analyzing.

The lowest level on the pyramid is the biological needs.

Level One: Biological Needs

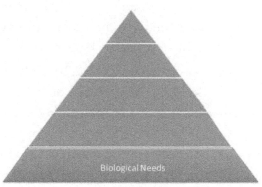

The biological needs form the base of the pyramid because these must be attended to before any of the others become relevant. This set of needs is concerned with one's physiological existence in the physical world. These include all of the elements necessary to stay alive and enjoy a decent quality of life:

- *Oxygen*
- *Water*
- *Protein*
- *Salt*
- *Ph balance*
- *Calcium, minerals, vitamins*
- *Be active*
- *Rest, sleep*
- *Get rid of waste*
- *Avoid pain*
- *Sex (continue the species)*

Even within this group, certain needs take precedence over others. For instance, if you were lost in the desert and found yourself both hungry and thirsty, but could only satisfy one of these needs, which would you choose?

It would make the most sense to first attempt to satisfy your thirst. Why? Aside from oxygen, water is the most important nutrient for the human body. You can live without food for weeks, but without water, your body will start to suffer serious negative consequences after only a couple of days. Lacking sufficient water, the body quickly becomes dehydrated. Dehydration causes the blood to thicken and lose volume, which causes the heart to work harder. In turn, one's physical and mental abilities are affected. Bottom line, unless your bodies stays properly hydrated, you will die, most unpleasantly. So, if you have to make a choice, choose water!

But what if you were dying of thirst and someone grabbed you by the throat and began to choke you? How important would that glass of water be to you then? Not so much. The need for oxygen is even stronger than the need for water. An oxygen-starved person doesn't need water because unless he has air to breathe. He'll be dead.

You'll undoubtedly recall the 2009 true story of Flight 1549, the plane that went down in the Hudson River. Imagine that during the takeoff, one of the passengers was thinking above the fiancé he was on the way to see, and their romantic dinner plans for the evening. A few minutes later, when that passenger was standing on a wing of the plane in the icy river, waiting for rescue, do you think those dinner plans would have been uppermost in his mind? Obviously not; there was at that moment a far more pressing need for him to satisfy.

There exists a hierarchy of needs. The most basic ones must be satisfied before others can be addressed.

Basic needs and handwriting

What happens when early in life the most basic needs of life have not been properly satisfied, not to a life-threatening degree, but poorly enough that we could say the child suffered from lack. There was not enough food to eat. Perhaps he came from a large family where he wasn't always noticed and had to fight his siblings for his basic needs. Or his parents were drug addicts who left him alone and without food for days at a time. Or the family was dirt poor and simply could not afford to provide enough for the children.

Often, the adult handwriting of someone whose most basic needs were neglected early on in life is undeveloped in its form. In cases where there physiological and mental damage occurs due to a lack of proper nutrients; the writing will have a childish appearance with slow speed.

In other cases, because writing movement and the lower zone are related to one's basic needs—food, sex, money, material goods—there may be extremes in lower zone length and width. The writer is seeking to fulfil those needs in a big way.

In some instances, such as the sample below, the handwriting may have a wild, "untamed" appearance. This is a 21-year-old male whose writing is a good example of undeveloped or disturbed form in one whose behavior is immature.

Disturbed form suggests very basic problems early in life. Notice in this sample how the form changes from print to script (erratic moods and attitudes), has slow speed (slow thinking), overly developed upper zone ("Do as I say, not as I do.") and is unattractive in its overall appearance (poorly developed ego).

The writer has changed the form from the copybook style he learned in school, indicating some originality, but it is not an improvement over copybook. Chances are, taking into consideration these various elements, he could very well have a learning disorder, such as ADHD.

sucks I am stuck in Hell with idiots in this class hope you can read this.

The writer is an underachiever who has not figured out how to learn from his mistakes. He does have something going for him: the spatial arrangement. With sufficient space between words and lines, despite having problems in other areas, such as the weak ego, he is actually able to maintain a decent perspective on how things fit in his life. That alone may allow him to function adequately in a lower level job.

"Form" is another word for writing style and is the equivalent of the choice of a computer font–copybook, simplified, elaborate, artistic, etc.

The next writer is a 25-year-old female who is alcohol-dependent and was arrested on a DUI charge. Leading graphologist Roger Rubin refers to overuse of alcohol (and other substances brought into the body) as "poisoned mother's milk" because it acts on an unconscious level as a substitute for the emotional and/or physical nourishment that the writer failed to receive at a very early stage of life.

To the best of my knowledge of hit another vehicle on this

The undeveloped writer acts childishly and has trouble adapting to new circumstances. She finds it difficult to open up to new ways of thinking; her worldview is a rather narrow one.

This handwriting is slow and premeditated. That is, the writer never makes a move without first calculating how it will benefit her. While she is not unintelligent, the form is poorly developed, revealing her weak ego. The emphasis on the middle zone at the expense of the other zones tells us that she fails to plan ahead and prefers to live in the moment, focusing on her most pressing needs.

With no upper zone to indicate a conscience and principles to live by, and a weak lower zone that avoids learning from the past, she is like a tree with no roots, blown this way and that by the circumstances in which she finds herself.

Next, we move up to the second level of Maslow's pyramid.

Level Two: Safety & Security Needs

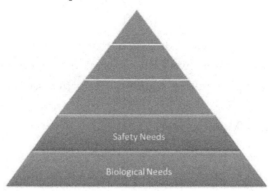

With the physiological needs satisfied, we are free to move up to the next level of needs, which is safety and security. These needs encompass several areas:

- *Safe living environment*
- *Structure*
- *Order*
- *Limits*
- *Job security*
- *Retirement plan*
- *Nest egg*
- *Insurance (health, car, home, etc.)*

Let's say you live in a great neighborhood where you are comfortable leaving your doors unlocked (hopefully, you do!). You've got plenty of money in the bank, and a great job, too. There's no reason for you to spend a lot of time and energy thinking about your safety and security needs because they are already met.

On the other hand, if you live in a ghetto in the Inner City and most nights when you go to bed gunshots in the street outside your bedroom window keep you awake, how can you think about anything other than how you are going to keep yourself and your family safe? Your need for safety and security is in the forefront of your mind all the time because that need is unmet.

You may have enough to eat and drink, but when you feel anxious and afraid you stay stuck at the second level of Maslow's pyramid.

Consider people who lived through World War II, especially those in European countries. After suffering terrible deprivation through those years, even though it is now more than a half-century later and they have everything they need, some continue to suffer from a nagging fear that there won't be enough food, or money to buy it. Consequently, they pinch pennies unnecessarily hard, or keep the pantry overstocked with food, just in case.

Hunger, neglect, abuse, death of a close family member, divorce. Significant problems in early childhood that interfere with getting one's need for safety and security met can cause the child to stay at those lower needs levels for a long time, in some cases, permanently. Living with lack impacts how a child perceives himself and the world throughout his lifetime.

If you are feeling anxious and afraid much of the time, your safety and security needs are making themselves known.

Safety and security needs in handwriting

The person who spends much of his life focused closely on the need for safety and security tends to adopt the slower arcade[2] as the predominant connective form. The slow arcade has long been interpreted by the graphological community as a primary sign of dishonesty. However, if we always keep in mind the surrounding elements the big picture–we will know that "dishonesty" doesn't necessarily mean stealing. It can be emotional dishonesty, where the writer is afraid to examine the truth of his past and is just fooling himself.

The arcade form provides a "safe arch" under which the writer can hide and protect himself. The slower arcade continually returns to the baseline, which represents the ground on which we stand, thus allowing the writer to stay in touch with (or keep his feet on) the ground for a sense of security.

The arcade is also "form-conscious," which means that external appearances are important to the writer. Behind the outer appearance of beauty, she hides her strong feelings of insecurity and a fear that "if you knew what I really looked like inside, you would hate me." So, she structures an outer image that reveals only what she wants others to see. On rare occasions when the mask slips and the truth comes out she feels humiliated. (Fast arcade writers also need security, but the need is manifested differently).

The three samples that follow demonstrate arcade forms written at slightly different speeds. Notice that they are all overly rounded because the slow arcade is rounded on the top. The letter "m" and "n" are the easiest place to see this.

In the first sample the writer has created a compact, or more accurately a crowded spatial arrangement. This is another indicator for fear and anxiety, where the writer needs to control all space, not letting anything or anyone else in. She may surround herself with the company of others or become overinvolved in work or other activities; anything to keep herself from having the time or, literally the space to just stop and breathe. In her mind, if she takes a step back, all hell will break loose.

Notice, in the first line she writes "I hope to secure a position". The word "secure" is very telling in this handwriting because security is exactly what she needs.

> In the next six months I hope to secure a position in a well established company that will allow me to grow and perform at my highest potential. I want this position to challenge my abilities and also give me the chance to learn new things. I want to be recognized for my good work and be able to advance up the ladder when possible.

The second sample is written even more slowly than the first. The writer has created such a strong outer mask that we can term this "persona writing." Each letter is carefully drawn. She's afraid to leave anything to chance, everything she does is calculated. In addition to the very slow arcades, the need to protect herself can be seen in ending strokes that rise into the upper zone and curve to the left. This movement is like an arm reaching up to cover the head in a defensive movement. The writer is stuck at the second level of the pyramid.

> There are many other differences that set us apart from others in the industry, we would appreciate the opportunity to explain it in full. I will follow up for an appointment.

In the third sample we find a combination of arcade and garland forms and the speed is very slightly faster. The need for safety and security is certainly present but is not as intensely expressed. The presence of the arcades suggests some emotional control to counteract the wavy baseline, which demonstrates her many emotional ups and downs.

The overall spatial arrangement is too crowded, which has a negative effect on her ability to plan ahead and work her plan. However, on the positive side, the large writing size, presence of a lower zone (albeit not a very well-proportioned one), and many curved strokes indicate a warm, friendly, outgoing person who can overcome some of the negatives.

Some graphologists teach that it is a bad idea to read the content of the sample. Since we are not crystal ball readers, however, reading the content can add important information

> The company seems to be very stable and profitable. The employees I met think very highly of it. Robert seems to be a very kind and easy going. He also is a very hardworking person that believes in his employees and rewards them for a job well done.

to the analysis. In the sample above, there are several telling words that are used by security-minded individuals: "stable," "hardworking," and "rewards."

While the arcade form used most by those whose safety and security needs relate to material and physical needs, such as health insurance, a good job, a stable situation, etc., there is another group of people who live on the safety and security needs level. The needs of this group have to do more with bad experiences they've had that make them afraid to be vulnerable, to expose themselves to anything new. Their fears are manifest through narrow, squeezed writing.

Narrow writing, rather than moving forward, pulls to the left (away from the future), which signifies fear and anxiety. The narrow writer has a deep fear of trying anything new and different. When he does reach out for new experiences he is likely to suffer intense stress. The writer of the following sample is a 35-year-old male who was raised in a very strict fundamentalist religion. His wife left him and he became involved with another woman, but due to his religious training that it was wrong to have a sexual relationship outside of marriage, he became so tormented by his conscience that he gave up the relationship after only a few weeks. His sense of safety and security came more from his religious ties than his relationship.

Notice the extremes in the upper and lower zone. Tall, narrow upper zones are often seen in handwritings of ultra-religious men (few women make an extremely tall upper zone) who behave hypocritically, making rules for their spouses, children, employees, but don't apply the same rules to themselves.

I'm really having to concentrate on this since I haven't done this in twenty years. I made a promise to myself in high school that I wouldn't ever write anything again. So you are witnessing history in this writing. I really...

When narrowness becomes extreme in a writing, or when a middle zone breaks down to formless thread, as in Richard Nixon's handwriting below, which we will consider next, paranoia is likely to be present.

I will be unable to attend the reception commemorating the fifth anniversary of Nightline

This note brings my congratulations & my...

His lack of feeling safe and secure is apparent in the flat, thready middle zone, which also reveals distrust of others. He feared revealing anything about himself and at least during the time when this sample was written, felt under a tremendous amount of stress and pressure.

In the next sample the overall form is narrow and angular. The writer, a 34-year-old male, would like to move forward (strong right slant) and try new experiences, but the narrowness and angles tells us that he constantly drives with the brakes on, so it takes him twice as long to get where he is going. He needs to feel as if he is in control in order to feel the sense

activities like backpacking, beach etc. I also like movies dancing fine dinning and the also like being a gentleman, and like working out. I till

of security he is basically lacking, and the idea of letting things just happen naturally just is too much for him to contemplate.

Level Three: Love and Belonging Needs

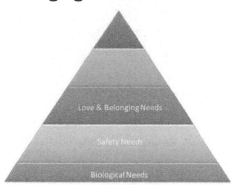

The third level of Maslow's pyramid is the need for love and belonging, which starts with the family of origin and spreads out into the community:

- *Family*
- *Friends*
- *Sweetheart/spouse*
- *Children*
- *Church*
- *Fraternity*
- *Community—service clubs, non-profit organizations*
- *Career—leads groups*
- *Clubs—crafts, reading, cooking, etc.*
- *Gangs*

The love and belonging needs are concerned with making a connection to others. This can include social stimulation, pleasure, and playtime, as well as giving back to the greater community as when we join civic groups and perform volunteer work.

Serving at a homeless shelter, for example, might fill some of one's needs for love and belonging.

> *When the need for love and belonging are not met, we become susceptible to loneliness and social anxiety.*

A child who feels unloved by her parents doesn't learn to love herself. As a result, she grows up looking for someone to love her. Unfortunately, she is likely to recreate in her relationships the same bad situation that she had early on.

She will be attracted to people who, in ways that she won't recognize, are very much like her parents. For example, a little girl has a mother who is so involved in her work that she fails to pay much attention to her child. It's not that the mother doesn't love the child in her own way, her priorities are simply elsewhere. The lonely little girl grows up and gets involved with men who at first appear warm and loving (unlike her mother), but once the relationship develops, they seem to change and manifest as emotionally cold, withdrawing their affections and support (like her mother).

Love and Belonging needs in handwriting

The handwriting of someone for whom the social and belonging needs are the strongest is usually soft and rounded with garland forms. The following three examples are very different from each other but have in common the strong need for love and belonging seen in rounded writing forms.

Below is the handwriting of Princess Diana, whose warm, affectionate personality was a well-known part of her public image. Her handwriting is soft and rounded, indicating her need for affection, attention, and approval. The clear spatial arrangement allowed her to function in the world, even when emotionally, she was desperately crying out for love and belonging.

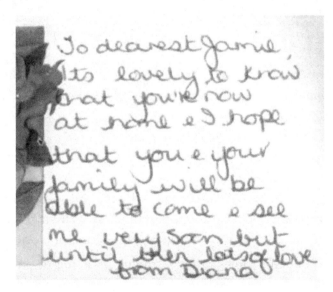

Nicole Brown Simpson, whose overly rounded handwriting appears next, contains more arcades than garlands, which demonstrates that her safety and security needs were as strong as her need for love and belonging. The writing is compact, the spatial arrangement weak[6], which negatively impacted her ability to be objective and see the whole picture. The need for love and belonging becomes so overwhelming that common sense takes a back seat. It is rare to see this type of handwriting where the writer has not been the victim of abuse in the so-called love relationships they draw into their lives.

The third example of rounded writing is that of Christine Falling, the child of a sixteen-year-old prostitute who could not meet her needs for love and belonging, and was, in fact, an abuser. She professed to enjoy babysitting and her clients thought highly of her, which undoubtedly satisfied some of those needs, until, over a period of time, she smothered six of them. Falling is currently serving a life sentence in Florida. Her handwriting contains some red flags for danger.

Note the flame-shaped upper loops, which is likely a manifestation of the head injury Falling suffered at the age of eight when her mother hit in the head with a two-by-four. These "X-formations" are sometimes seen in the handwritings of many people who feel guilty about a death close to them.

Princess Diana, Nicole Brown Simpson, and Christine Falling had in common that they were motivated by their unmet needs for love and belonging. There are important differences, though. Although all three have large middle zones and are overly rounded in their form, Falling's handwriting contains those important red flags for danger. Falling's handwriting could not predict that she would kill those she loved, but the roundedness of it reveals the depth of her need to be loved and to belong to somebody.

Those whose handwriting is overly rounded in their form are stuck on the third level of Maslow's pyramid.

Level Four: Esteem Needs

The fourth needs level identified by Maslow is the esteem needs, of which there are two varieties.

Lower esteem needs come from *outside* oneself:

- *Fame*
- *Glory*
- *Status*
- *Recognition*
- *Attention*
- *Reputation*
- *Appreciation*
- *Dominance.*

Higher esteem needs come from *inside*:

- *Self-respect*
- *Inner confidence*
- *Competence*
- *Achievement*

- *Mastery*
- *Independence*
- *Freedom*

In the first case, the person needs to be in the spotlight and have others looking up to him, fawning over him, admiring him. The good opinion of others is more important than just about anything else.

In the second case, his own good opinion of himself matters most. This person works hard to do a good job because it's the right thing to do, not for the admiration, or even adulation it might bring. It might take owning a big house and a fancy car for those with lower level esteem needs to feel good about themselves—they require external trappings of success. Someone with higher level esteem needs could live in a grass hut with very little in the way of material possessions, yet still have strong self-confidence. Note, however, that this doesn't make that one a "good" person, nor the one stuck at the lower level a "bad" person.

Maslow agreed with Alfred Adler, founder of the school of individual or self-psychology, that low self-esteem and inferiority complexes are at the root of most psychological problems.

Handwriting and Esteem Needs

The handwriting of someone who is motivated by their higher-level esteem needs is likely to be slightly larger than average in size and have well-developed capitals that are approximately 2-3 times larger than the middle zone height. The zones should be proportionate (sometimes the lower zone will be emphasized in length and width), there will be rightward trend and strong rhythm.

In the case of one who is stuck at lower level esteem needs, the capitals will be bloated and perhaps elaborate, but unattractive. The basic rhythm is likely to be disturbed.

Diet guru Jenny Craig's handwriting shows strong esteem needs that are met in positive ways. The strong, balanced rhythm, colorful pressure, and rightward trend indicate one who believes in herself. She can be a steamroller when it comes to getting her needs met; nothing will stand in her way.

Notice the hook at the end of the final stroke in "and," which is a testament to her unwillingness to let go. Her signature is strong and bold, and all the capitals are tall and well-formed. She has a big image of herself, and the wherewithal to make it work. She is motivated by her esteem needs.

Then set high goals work hard and don't quit until you achieve each one.

Jenny Craig

The same is true of business mogul Donald Trump, whose bold block printing defies anyone to oppose him. His signature is a series of sharp, heavy angles. There is no arguing that Trump's esteem needs motivate him and make him who he is, a supremely self-assured person whose self-belief that he would make a good leader of the country helped put him in office. He habitually writes at an angle, which tells us that he is not going to follow somebody else's rules, he makes his own.

Note: Trump's handwriting has remained consistent over at least thirty years.

The following sample demonstrates someone who is motivated by his lower esteem needs. The form, the rhythm (which is part of the writing movement), and the spatial arrangement are all disturbed.

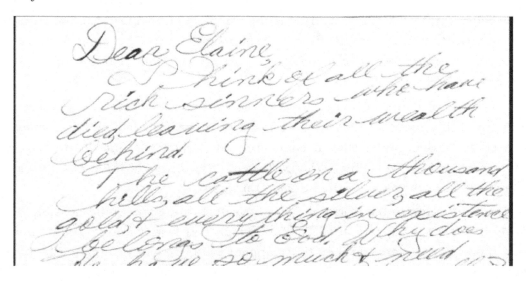

The writer, a male in his 30's, has poor self-esteem, but the capital letters, and especially the PPI, are overly elaborate and poorly formed, drawing attention to them, which suggests that he overcompensates for his lack of confidence and his weak ego by coming on too strong. The fact that the handwriting form is so poorly developed and rounded (unusual in a male) indicates that the writer's needs were neglected at several different levels.

Next up is another example of one who projects a big, though not strong, self-image with the large size and big, attention-drawing elaborate capitals, but who lacks confidence based on any real self-esteem.

The writing is crowded and lacks the perspective of space. The rhythm is poor and the letter designs (form) is undeveloped. This sample was taken from a letter written by a stalker to a celebrity.

Deficit Needs

When you have all you need of something, you don't feel anything at all. The need is no longer a motivator for you. If you have plenty to eat, you don't need to spend a lot of time thinking about your next meal. If you are in a warm, loving relationship, you don't need to think about lack of affection. If you have a good job and a decent place to live, you don't need to worry about money.

A deficit, on the other hand, is when you don't have enough of something, there is a lack. We hear a lot about the budget deficit, where the government claims it lacks enough money to function properly. The four levels of need that we've just discussed—the physiological, safety and security, love and belonging, and esteem needs—were termed by Maslow "Deficit needs" or "D-Needs." When one of those needs is not met, you feel it like an itchy rash begging to be scratched, and it will continue begging until you find some relief.

The fact is, a deficit in any important area motivates you to expend your energy trying to satisfy the need. If your personal bank account is empty and the monthly bills are coming due, the deficit makes itself painfully felt. You are motivated to seek work or borrow money or do whatever you can to satisfy the need.

What happens when things change?

When it gets too cold in your home, the thermostat switches on the heater. When it gets too warm, the thermostat switches it off. This is the principle of homeostasis: the tendency of a system to maintain its internal stability. Your brain acts the same way as the thermostat. If your body temperature is too warm, you take off some clothes and if you're too cool, you put more clothes on.

Maslow applied the principle of homeostasis to the various needs levels we've discussed so far. These are all instinctual needs that we begin to recognize early in life. Babies cry when they need to be fed, when they need to feel safe, when they need attention and affection, etc. These are all "D needs." When a D need arises, the brain feels a hunger to satisfy it. When the need is satisfied, the hunger stops.

So, what if you're on top of the world and you have everything you could possibly need, but something unforeseen happens and all of a sudden you lose it and you find yourself under stress in one or more areas. When that happens, you are likely to regress to a lower level of functioning.

Let's say you had a great career and now your company has suddenly downsized and you're out of a job. Without warning you find yourself feeling horribly anxious and insecure.

In the Ben Affleck movie, The Company Men, we see a perfect illustration of such a situation. Affleck's character, Bobby Walker, is highly successful at his job. He's been with the company a long time. He's got a good relationship with the boss, a nice wife, a great kid, a big house and a Porsche. His self-esteem is high, he knows he's got it made. Then he's hit in a round of layoffs and Bobby is totally unprepared.

As the money runs out and he can't pay the bills, he is eventually forced to take a job with his brother-in-law, who he doesn't like, but who owns a small construction company. Unaccustomed to manual labor, Bobby makes a moderate descent to a lower level of functioning. Over time, he's able to make the necessary adjustments to his new status. Another character in the film, though, is so tied up in what he does—he is his job—that when he is unexpectedly laid off, too, he can't handle it. He loses his sense of self (lower esteem needs) and takes drastic action.

Maybe you got a sub-prime mortgage and now your house is under water and all you can think about is how to get some money (security needs) to live on. Or the spouse to whom you gave the best twenty years of your life decides out of the blue to find someone else and leaves you. For the first time in years, you're focusing on your need for love because you no longer have it in your life (belonging needs).

Or you have a great marriage, but when you were young, your father cheated on your mother and as an adult you constantly worry that your spouse is going to leave you (security and belonging needs). In times like these, you regress to a lower needs level because once again, the D needs are making themselves felt.

We can also see D needs demonstrated as a society. When 9/11 happened, the entire country experienced an unfamiliar sense of insecurity and anxiety, and as a result became focused on security above all else. In a natural emergency such as an earthquake, a hurricane, tornado, tsunami, where food is no longer being regularly being delivered to grocery stores, or you have to line up for bottles of water, you suddenly have to start thinking about where your next meal is coming from. Are you feeling anxious yet?! The point is, one's needs can change abruptly, and when they do, we follow the natural tendency to seek homeostasis, which provides a level of comfort.

Deficit needs are about something that is lacking

Maslow named five levels of functioning, of which we have discussed the lower four. The fifth, self-actualization, will be discussed later in this paper. Meanwhile, let's look at some more examples of various needs levels.

Randy is 32. She wasn't starved or beaten—her physiological needs were met, but as a child, she didn't feel safe or loved, and for good reason. This young woman tells the story of her own mother's attempt to kill her and her young sisters. What in her handwriting tells us that she is stuck at the safety and security and also the esteem needs level?

The pictures of movement and form and space are all disturbed, seen in the variability of spacing, size, letter forms, and a lack of control in the movement. The overall linear style gives the writing a masculine appearance, which makes sense. Because she was devastated by the way she had been treated by the women in her young life, Randy changed her appearance to make herself look like a boy, and her handwriting has a masculine appearance, too. The writing could use some curved forms for better balance.

> the underlying problems. At about age 3
> or 4 my mother tried to kill my sisters and
> I. The state placed us in a foster at
> age 5. And there I went through 8 years
> of verbal abuse. I've always felt rejected
> unwanted, and unlovable. Somewhere along
> the line I built walls and put on mask
> to hide me. This began when I was
> real young. One of the walls and/or mask

The simplifications reveal her innate intelligence, but she's been an underachiever most of her life. Her behavior has been unpredictable, impulsive, and anxious. She used drugs and alcohol to fill herself up. Happily, she is now working on getting her life together.

The next sample was written by a 27-year-old woman. Gin started using drugs at the age of age 13 and soon became a prostitute. The writing looks like a young teenager, and this is where Gin became emotionally stuck. She's now working on turning her life around but has endured many painful experiences because of her addictions. Her children were removed from her care, but she worked hard and got them back.

At what needs level does her handwriting suggest Gin lives? The rounded quality of the writing indicates that love and affection are problem areas for her. That's what she's always looking for and feels as if she can never get enough.

recovering drug addict, alcoholic, sex addic
and over eater. These are just to name a
few addiction I have battled in my life.
I started using drugs when I was 13
and moved to using sex to get what I
wanted and needed to Survive as I
lived on the streets as a runaway fro
home. I started my Criminal life at
13 as well, going in and out of

Casey Anthony

We will now explore a sample written by Casey Anthony, the young mother who, in 2006, was acquitted of murdering her toddler, Caylee.

The most obvious issue is the weak picture of space (everything crowded together). She wrote on lined paper, but the writing, which has been reduced here to fit, takes up all the space and leaves no breathing room. There is no room perspective or listening to what others have to say. The writer imposes herself on the environment and cannot see the forest for the trees. Without an upper zone, we could say that she has poor reality testing. She makes her own rules and respects no one.

The roundedness (slower arcades) indicates a total focus on feeding her needs from the outside. Despite the overall large size, her ego is weak and needs constant puffing up. Her emotional development was arrested at a very young age. It may be that she was not given sufficient opportunity as she was growing up to handle disappointments on her own. During her trial she accused her father and her brother of molesting her in childhood. Both denied the charges.

Casey sees herself as the center of the universe and believes that the world revolves around her. Her need for love and belonging is a bottomless pit, as is her need for safety. Notice how the letters hug the baseline (need for safety and security). Although the large size suggests that she comes on strong, the squeezed compactness of the picture of space tells us that inside she feels weak and powerless.

So, I luce have this super cool pen, and its blue! Thanks for my newest contra band! I have to get used to having something so sturdy to write with. You should see my try to sign something with a regular pen, and add handcuffs - its comical. The boys always have a good laugh at my expense, I mean, with me. Ha! I can't believe how much we've written in just a few days. That's what happens when one, or two in our case, is starved to open and honest and unsensored conversation. I definitely agree with you about everything, especially the horrible feeling of betrayal and not wanting to ever betray someone you care about. We've both had to deal with a lot of that since

What made Casey Anthony who she is? Let's examine her parents' handwriting.

Casey's mother, Cindy, has been variously described as a control freak, a narcissist, and an ice queen. None of that appears in her handwriting. What we do see, however, is a "good girl" who wants to keep everything nice; doesn't want to upset the applecart. She is willing to keep whatever secrets she needs to in order to keep the peace.

you you. + you you...
ever. You know how much you have
always meant to me.
      Please take care of yourself.
              Love always
                 mom.

A perfectionist, Cindy avoids the emotional truth—note the double-joined ovals (emotional dishonesty). The circle go all the way around before moving forward, which indicates one who avoids directly facing emotional issues, and just talks around them. Notice, too, the "o" in the word "Mom." The little bow tie is symbolic of locking one's lips and refusing to part with certain information. As long as things look nice on the outside, Cindy is okay. Or so she would like to believe.

Following are two samples written by Casey's father, George Anthony. The tough, block printed style is probably a leftover from his days as a police detective. It is remarkable in its difference from his cursive writing, which has an almost feminine quality. Yet, both writings have in common a strong need for control.

only for a few moments. We can only talk about what you want to discuss. It has been too long for not being able to hear your voice, call me "Papa Joe, Dad. I need to hear that from you, no matter what. Please Casey, let Papa Joe / Dad come to visit. You can make it happen, you are the Boss. So what if

JUST WANTED TO WRITE YOU A FEW LINES TO LET YOU KNOW "I LOVE YOU".

SINCE THE LAST TIME I WROTE, WHICH WAS ABOUT 3 WEEKS AGO, I GUESS I HAVE COME TO ACCEPT THAT YOU DO NOT WANT TO SEE ME. FOR REASONS THAT I DO NOT UNDERSTAND, NOR CAN I TRY TO COMPREHEND, I AM FORCED TO LIVE WHAT IS LEFT OF MY LIFE, EMPTY.

Both are highly regular and tight. Maintaining that degree of regularity takes a lot of energy and focus. His motivation comes from the need to protect himself, the need for security, and his esteem needs. George's handwriting cannot reveal whether Casey's accusation that he molested her is true or not, but it does show perfectionism and a propensity for covering up anything that makes him look less than his best.

The writer of the sample below, in her mid-twenties, is the director of a children's choir and a classically trained opera singer. Her illegible signature is encircled by the final "y," which suggests a need to protect her feelings about her father, who left the family when she was a young teen. Her handwriting is highly creative with quick, fluid forms.

The organization is good, the spatial arrangement a little wide—she likes plenty of her own personal space. The simplification and flexibility allow her to jump rapidly from one thing to another. She is motivated by her esteem needs.

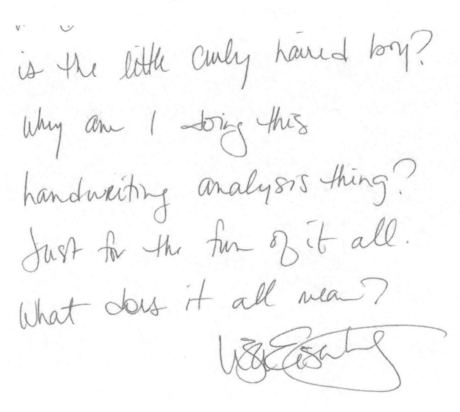

Finally, we come to the highest level on Maslow's needs pyramid: Self-actualization.

Self-Actualization

The needs on the fifth level are of a different variety than the four lower level D needs. These are more abstract and spiritual in nature. Maslow called them the Growth motivation or Metaneeds because they go above and beyond the ordinary basic needs. He termed the highest level the B-needs, Being Needs, or self-actualization, which is all about fulfilling your highest potential. Think of that old army slogan: Be all you can be.

The principle of homeostasis that we learned works with the D-needs (when the deficit is satisfied, the need goes away) does not work the same way with the Being needs. Once the B needs make themselves felt, they just keep getting stronger and the more you fulfil them, the stronger they get. Maslow believed it is so difficult to fulfill your potentials, that only about 2 percent of people ever became truly self-actualized.

Later researchers took issue with Maslow's theory, and not all psychologists agree that the lower needs must be taken care of before self-actualization can be realized. Certainly, there have been great artists, composers, poets, etc., who came from desperate circumstances where their lower needs were not met, yet they managed to reach beyond and fulfil their potential, so it's probably not realistic to be a purist about it. Still, Maslow's hierarchy of needs provides a sort of typology for handwriting analysts to add one more tool to their toolbox. If it works for you, use it.

Traits of the self-actualized person

Maslow identified a number of traits that defined self-actualized people:

— *Reality-centered: they can tell the difference between what's fake and what's real and genuine.*

— *Problem-centered: they view life's difficulties as problems that demand a solution, not just give up. They are proactive rather than reactive.*

— *The ends don't necessarily justify the means: the means (the journey) may be more important than the ends.*

— *Comfortable being alone: relatively independent of culture and environment; rely on personal experiences and judgment (not susceptible to social pressure).*

— *Open to ethnic variety: treasure differences (basic democratic values).*

— *Quality over quantity: intimate personal relations with a few close friends, rather than shallow relationships with many.*

— *Unhostile sense of humor: never directing unkind humor at others.*

— *Acceptance of self and others: they take you as you are, not as they would like you to be.*

— *Spontaneity and simplicity: lacking in artifice or pretension, not putting on airs.*

— *Sense of wonder: able to see things with a childlike wonder (ability to be creative, inventive, original)*

— *Peak experiences: an experience that takes you out of yourself and makes you feel very tiny, or at one with life/nature/god—you feel you are part of the infinite, the eternal. These experiences change people for the better. Some call them mystical experiences.*

From that description, you would think self-actualized people were perfect. Of course, they're not. It seems highly unlikely that anyone can manifest all of those traits all the time. Maslow noted that problems arose when self-actualized people failed to get their Metaneeds met. In fact, under those circumstance, several flaws emerged:

- *Realistic anxiety and guilt*
- *Absentmindedness*
- *Overly kind*
- *Some experienced moments of ruthlessness, surgical coldness, loss of humor.*

When forced to live apart from the values they hold dear, they experienced depression, despair, disgust, alienation and cynicism. Not that one has to be a disappointed self-actualizer to experience these feelings!

The handwriting of self-actualized people

In 1943, Maslow selected a number of well-known people to study self-actualization. While he realized that he was using just a small group to test his theory, he viewed it more or less as a pilot study, just a start that he hoped others would build on. He felt that the people he selected were "exemplary" and met his high standard for Being needs. In making his selection, he examined their backgrounds, their writings, their deeds, and what other information was available about them.

It may be assumed that Maslow probably wasn't looking at their handwriting when he chose the people he included in the study. However, the group of personality traits he felt were representative of these people show up as similar handwriting characteristics in the global sense (not in a "this means that" sense).

Given the cluster of personality traits common to self-actualized people as described above, what would we expect their handwritings to look like?

The following handwriting characteristics reflect, in general, the personality traits described by Maslow:
- ✓ *Good distribution of space*
- ✓ *Simplified form*
- ✓ *Strong rhythm*
- ✓ *Originality*
- ✓ *Rightward trend*
- ✓ *Moderate to fast speed*
- ✓ *Balance of connective forms*

Let's look at some of the people Maslow included in his study and their handwriting and see whether this list holds true.

Abraham Lincoln (1809-1865)

16th president, four years in office.

Lincoln's handwriting as seen on the following page is dynamic but not dictatorial. It has excellent rhythm (ebb and flow) and forward movement (right trend). He wrote with fast speed, reflecting a quick thinker who is able to move from one project to another without undue stress.

We see a good mix of connective forms—some thread for flexibility and adaptability. The interesting combinations (ex. "wh" in "who") allowed him to intuit and quickly pick up on the mood of a room without waiting to collect a lot of facts and data.

The writing does not conform strictly to the copybook of the day, but has plenty of originality, which indicates that Lincoln was not the type to stick with tried and true methods just because things had always been done that way. Instead, he was able to use his considerable resourcefulness to find more effective means of operating.

The spatial arrangement is clear and well laid out, though the right margin is quite narrow, suggesting his eagerness to move forward.

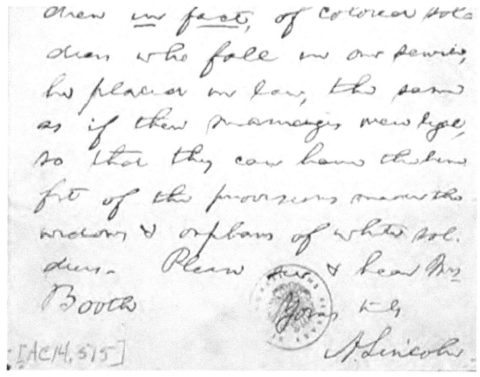

Eleanor Roosevelt (1884-1962)

Civil rights advocate, enhanced the status of working women (she opposed the Equal Rights Amendment, believing it would adversely affect women), she would have made a terrific executive. From her intense, driven, handwriting, she could have been President! Roosevelt was a go-getter. Notice the rightward movement, strong rhythm and good spatial arrangement.

Albert Einstein (1879-1955)

Theoretical physicist, won the 1921 Nobel Prize in physics (quantum theory)

The handwriting has forward, progressive movement, strong rhythm, rightward trend. The spatial arrangement is fairly close, but that may be due to the small writing space, and the writing is overall positive with simplified forms.

113

Jane Addams (1860-1935)

The first woman to receive Nobel Peace Prize, she died on the day it was awarded to her. A feminist by philosophy, a humanitarian in an underprivileged area of Chicago. Founder of Hull House, which still exists to help the community.

A leader in woman's suffrage, Wikipedia says she shared a "romantic friendship" with a woman, which must have been challenging in that era. As a child, she developed tuberculosis of the spine, which probably affected her handwriting, which is thready, with a downward slope.

Along with her health problems, Addams was a very busy woman who operated under a great deal of stress. The writing is highly simplified, written fast. It is original, not following the copybook of the times, and has strong rightward movement. The baseline is concave, pulling itself up to finish what it starts.

Frederick Douglass (1818-1895)

Born a slave, Douglass became a statesman who believed in the equality of all. A social reformer, brilliant orator, writer (wrote several autobiographies). Douglass lived at a time when slave owners claimed that slaves didn't have the intellectual capacity to function as independent American citizens. He proved them dead wrong.

He actively supported women's suffrage and strongly believed in the equality of all. After the civil war he worked on behalf of equal rights for freedmen and held multiple public offices. A favorite saying of his was, *"I would unite with anybody to do right and with nobody to do wrong."*

Especially considering the challenges he faced as a child learning to read and write at a time when it was forbidden, his handwriting is really high form level with dynamic, strong rightward movement and simplification.

Aldous Huxley (1894-1963)

The Huxley family had members who excelled in scientific, medical, artistic, and literary field. Several members occupied senior public positions in the UK. Aldous' mother died when he was 14. Three years later he had an illness that left him nearly blind for 2-3 years.

Best known for his book Brave New World, which addressed the dehumanizing aspects of scientific progress (society operates on principles of mass production and Pavlovian conditioning—what would he say about Facebook?!). He was a Hollywood screenwriter in the 1930s (Pride and Prejudice, Jane Eyre) and had the distinction of his version of Alice In Wonderland being rejected by Walt Disney, who said "I can only understand every third word."

A humanist and a pacifist, he was interested in parapsychology and philosophical mysticism. He took psychedelic drugs (it was thought that his characterization of the caterpillar in Alice came from his experiments with psychedelic drugs) and was considered a leader of modern thought. On his deathbed he requested LSD, which his wife gave him (he died a few hours after JFK's assassination).

From a graphological standpoint his handwriting is quite beautiful, with its open, airy spatial arrangement and bouncy, light rhythm. Highly original, simplified, it is progressive, it moves forward.

116

Thomas Jefferson (1743-1826)

Known as one of the greatest US Presidents and principle author of Declaration of Independence. His handwriting is extraordinary in its organization. It retains its regularity, with some simplification. Even without the same kind of dynamic movement as the other writings we have seen, there is an inexorability in the way it moves across the page.

Felix Klein (1911-1994)

Graphologist and highly respected teacher in the field of handwriting analysis.

Began studying handwriting analysis at age 13 in Vienna. During World War II Felix Klein was imprisoned in Dachau and Buchenwald for nearly a year. There, he developed his theory of directional pressure (strokes that otherwise would be straight are curved), which came from his observation that prisoners whose handwriting showed greater flexibility were the ones who were more likely to survive the brutality they faced in the camps.

In 1940, after a year in London, he emigrated to New York and became a watchmaker, beginning his handwriting analysis business in 1969. Many handwriting analysts personally experienced Felix' kindness and generosity in sharing his knowledge.

17.) Is the Occupation of special importance to society?

18.) At what age are workers considered "through"

19.) How may the occupation be rated as a way of life?

His handwriting fits very well with the other self-actualized people we've reviewed with its strong rightward movement, highly simplified and original. The rhythm is slightly disturbed, which may have been a function of his age (he was in his 80s at the time of writing). But age notwithstanding, there is strong dynamism in the writing.

Becoming self-actualized

There is a group of behaviors that can lead to self-actualization, and they're not rocket science to achieve. If you want to stretch beyond who you are and reach out for greater things, practice these:

> *(a) Live in the here and now: Experience life like a child, with full absorption and concentration;*
>
> *(b) Try new things instead of sticking to safe paths;*
>
> *(c) Listen to your own feelings in evaluating experiences instead of the voice of tradition or authority or the majority;*
>
> *(d) Avoid pretense ('game playing') and be honest;*
>
> *(e) Be prepared to be unpopular if your views don't coincide with those of the majority;*
>
> *(f) Take responsibility and work hard;*
>
> *(g) Identify your defenses; have the courage to give them up.*

For more information about Abraham Maslow and his theories:
http://webspace.ship.edu/cgboer/maslow.html

This page intentionally left blank

How to find personality traits in handwriting using the gestalt method

By Sheila R. Lowe, C.G, M.S., Psy.

© How to find personality traits in handwriting using the gestalt method Sheila Lowe 2011

www.sheilalowe.com

sheila@sheilalowe.com

(805) 658-0109

Introduction

This paper assumes that the reader is familiar with the gestalt principles of Spatial Arrangement, Writing Form, and Writing Movement as taught in my self-study course. A very brief overview appears on the next page.

The handwriting indicators in this monograph are intended to offer a general picture for each personality trait and is not an exhaustive list. You will see some of the handwriting elements that are listed for a trait in the handwriting you are analyzing, but you won't necessarily see all of them in one sample. On the other hand, you may be of the opinion that there are other indicators not listed, but which could be included.

As always, look at the writing as a whole before making any interpretation as to a particular trait. You will find some overlap in personality traits and their definitions.

Each trait is seen along a spectrum from strong to weak. As you begin your analysis, ask yourself at which segment of the spectrum a particular trait may fall. In many cases, the rhythm of movement will be especially important in answering that question. For example, you might see the trait of self-esteem in the writing you are analyzing. Self-esteem in reasonable supply exists at the middle of the Esteem spectrum and is a positive trait. However, as it moves further along the spectrum it turns into self-aggrandizement. The same handwriting characteristics would apply, but in self-aggrandizing, they are taken to extremes. This is true of most, if not all, traits, so you must determine how weak or strong they are and make an interpretation accordingly.

The gestalt "pictures"

"Gestalt" is defined as *"a configuration or pattern of elements so unified as a whole that it cannot be described merely as a sum of its parts."*

Some methods of handwriting analysis build a picture of personality by minutely examining individual elements of the writing. The gestalt method views the handwriting as a whole picture that is greater than the sum of its parts. "Gestalt" can be applied thus: a handwriting that has a good gestalt looks pretty good and is well-balanced, attractive. It will not be perfect, but it doesn't need anything added or taken away to make it look better. On the other hand, you will know when a handwriting does not have a good gestalt because when you look at it, you immediately see (or sense) that "something is wrong." But what?

You will be able to understand what area(s) of personality manifest problems by analyzing which areas of the handwriting sample are out of balance: the spatial arrangement, the writing form, or the writing movement.

For the purposes of this paper, which is an extra lesson to my gestalt course, I will speak only in broad generalities here as a review.

Using the gestalt method, we are looking at the whole handwriting and we know that all the parts are intertwined, but we are able to analyze the three major aspects or "big pictures":

The *picture of space* or *spatial arrangement* of the writing indicates how well the writer organizes his life and time, how he behaves socially, and his thought processes. The *picture of form* tells you about the state of his ego, and the *picture of movement* gives you information about the basic energy available to do the work of the personality.

A strong picture of space, form, and/or movement means the writing looks balanced in those areas. One, two, or all three of these areas may be out of balance. If the writing is crowded, the picture of space is weak. If there are sudden large spaces between words, the picture of space is disturbed. In either case, the writer has problems with planning, with intellectual processes (reasoning, understanding, etc.) and/or with social skills.

If the writing is copybook style, the picture of form is weak. If the letter forms are undeveloped or unattractive, the picture of form is disturbed. In either case, there's a problem with the writer's ego.

If the overall rhythm is either slack or monotonous, the picture of movement is weak. If the rhythm is jumpy and nervous, the picture of movement is disturbed. In either case, the problem is with the writer's basic energy.

Everyone suffers internal conflicts at one time or another. Sometimes we are faced with bad habits that we know we should stop, but for a variety of reasons don't want to, and that sets up an internal conflict. For example, someone who is addicted to drugs or alcohol may not want to give them up because of the pleasurable feelings he gets from them. They push aside the bad aspects of the usage and forget the hangover or the sickness. Or he may believe that he just can't do it even though he might want to.

The same can be true of unhealthy relationships. Perhaps you recognize that your partner is abusing you, but because there are still some good parts to the relationship, you stay and focus only on the good, ignoring the bad behavior of your partner. There is an internal struggle between the dissatisfaction with that life and the love for the partner.

EGO STRENGTH

Internal Conflicts	
Descriptive words:	Confusion, disharmony, dissonance, clash, friction.

Handwriting: *zonal interference (lower loops hanging down and clashing with the upper loops on the next line), weak (crowded) or disturbed (wide word spaces) spatial arrangement, narrow margins, persona writing style.*

Following is just one example of someone suffering from inner conflicts. As you will see, his writing has several characteristics as described above. There are, however, many manifestations of this trait, so other writings might look completely different and have other handwriting characteristics (such as disturbed space).

The writing has a weak spatial arrangement. Although this is an intelligent person, he is unable to separate himself from his problems and stand back to look at life objectively. Everything is too crowded, too jammed together. He can't see the forest for the trees.

Self-Esteem	
Descriptive words:	(High self-esteem) confidence, dignity, self-assurance, self-regard, self-respect, a sense of worth.

Self-esteem relates to how you feel about yourself, how much space you believe you deserve to take up in the world. Strong self-esteem means that you like and respect yourself, while low self-esteem means that you don't.

The personality trait of self-esteem relates to many areas of life, including how you feel about your job, your social standing, what you see as your strengths. People with high self-esteem tend to be more confident, happy, and more motivated to succeed more than those with low self-esteem.

Handwriting: *(High self-esteem) strong rhythm, capitals 2-3 times the middle zone height, simplification, PPI twice the middle zone height, combined letter forms, clear spatial arrangement, good proportion of width/height in middle zone and between middle and upper and lower zones.*

The next sample was written by a woman with strong self-esteem. Her simplified PPI is sized proportionately to the middle zone height.

You can feel the energy bristling in the writing rhythm, as her energy moves outward, toward other people. Her word spacing is a tiny bit close, but not so close as to make her intrusive. The lower zone is full and inclusive of others, and there is a combination of connective forms, which indicates the ability to interact with people of all types, not just those who are like her.

Self-aggrandizing (vain)	
Descriptive words:	**audacious, brazen, cheeky, cocksure, impertinent, arrogant, presumptuous, rude, thoughtless, egotistical, big-headed, pompous, self-applauding, full of hot air, know-it-all, loudmouth, puffed-up, boastful, grandiosity, affectation, narcissistic, self-worshiping, vainglorious, conceited, selfish.**

When self-esteem goes to extremes, it becomes self-aggrandizement or vanity. The vain person has an overarching belief in himself and his abilities. He thinks he is so special that nobody else can understand him. He makes grandiose claims about his supposed or real accomplishments, believing that he is more important than you are. He lives in his own little world where he can enjoy his fantasies of great success and superiority.

This a narcissist whose energy is channeled into exaggerating his own importance. He wants to be seen as more powerful than he really is, and he overcompensates by coming on too strong. Afraid that others won't see him as confident and powerful, he takes steps to make sure everyone knows it.

There is a need for constant attention, yet he finds it impossible to maintain close personal relationships because others are exhausted (or disgusted) by his need for worshipful behavior. Because this person is so egotistical and more concerned about how he looks, he tends to be low in empathy for others and often alienates those who might otherwise have been friends. His egotism is seen, not in a large middle zone, but in an overdeveloped upper zone, often to the neglect of the middle and lower zones.

A writer with the trait of vanity might be diagnosed as having Narcissistic Personality Disorder.

> **Handwriting:** *extremely tall upper zone and capitals (more than 3x mzh), narrow letter forms, persona writing style, large attention-drawing hooks in the upper zone. Vastly overblown capital letters, crowded (weak) spatial arrangement, first letter in a word (not a capital letter) is larger than the rest, last letter in a word increases in size, some forms of persona writing.*

The sample above has a disproportionately tall upper zone, narrow and retraced letters, and has extremely light pressure (pressure was darkened here for purposes of illustration). In this case, it is the upper zone that is the red flag for vanity. Note that his spatial arrangement is clear, so despite the problem we see in the poor zonal distribution, he is able to function in the world. This is a 34-year-old left-handed male with an authoritarian personality. He expects others to look up to him and obey his directives without question ("do as I say, not as I do.").

Self-assertive		
Descriptive words:		bold, confident, effervescent, vivacious, self-assured, strong.

A self-assertive person knows how to get his needs met in a direct manner. The trick is to know when to stop before that direct manner becomes aggressiveness. This has to do with understanding appropriate boundaries.

Those who are self-assertive are able to defend themselves in the face of attack, using strength but not acting aggressively. Aggressive behavior violates the boundaries of others.

Great leaders possess this quality, using non-violent resistance rather than aggressively rolling over others.

> **Handwriting:** *strong rhythm, strong right trend, well-developed capital letters and PPI, firm baseline, medium-moderately heavy pressure, speed, high degree of connectedness, some angular forms, clear letter and word spacing, block printing.*

The writing below in Figure 4 is block printed with strong right trend, speed, and clear spacing. The writer is a 50-year-old right-handed male. It is further along the spectrum toward the aggressive end, but there are not enough angular forms to interpret it quite that strongly. However, the variability in the letter size and low self-control indicates that he can suddenly become aggressive in certain situations.

Aggressive		
Descriptive words:		(cocky, sassy, tough, bellicose, domineering, imperious, militant, contentious, disruptive, intrusive, offensive, quarrelsome, threatening, pugnacious.

Aggressiveness becomes an extreme of Assertiveness. Psychologist Karen Horney described this type as "moving against" other people. In other words, the aggressive person he prefers to push for what he wants, rather than "making nice." He's argumentative and leads with his chin. He wants everyone to know who he is and that he's going to get what he wants, no matter what. Interestingly, he has no respect for those who don't stand up to him.

You can expect him to be ruthless and competitive, desiring to win at all costs, often bullying his way into getting what he wants. The person with a strong Aggressive trait might be diagnosed with Antisocial Personality Disorder.

Robert ("Bobby Joe") Long (below) is a serial killer on death row in Florida. With its high degree of angles, muddy quality and extreme t-crosses, his handwriting is aggressive to the extreme.

Handwriting: *high degree of angles with strong right slant; straight strokes, tics on initial strokes, long, heavy t-crosses, down slanted t-crosses, muddy ductus, tall initial stroke on "p." The person who chooses to write with red ink adds to this trait, as do heavy cross-outs.*

Humility	
Descriptive words:	gentle, courteous, modest, obliging, ordinary, quiet, reserved, shy, soft-spoken, unpretentious, politely submissive, respectful of others.

Humility should not be confused with low self-esteem but has more to do with modesty. The best leaders are humble, not boastful or drawing undue attention to themselves, but respecting others and putting them first. Opposite of the vain person, the humble one does not thrive on recognition and acclaim, but instead, promotes the good of others.

Handwriting: *medium-small overall size, simplification, plain capital letters, balanced zones.*

Next is an example of humility. The writing is modest and balanced, with small capitals. It doesn't draw attention to itself. With the high degree of garland forms, this is not someone you could imagine yelling and screaming when they are upset. Soft-spoken and kind, almost to the point of finding it difficult to express negative emotions directly.

Integrity		
Descriptive words:		sincerity, candor, forthrightness, honesty, honorableness, incorruptibility, principled, rectitude, virtue, purity, straightforwardness.

Integrity is the willingness to be who you say you are, to do what you say you will do. Someone with high integrity will make sacrifices if necessary in order to keep his word. He doesn't worry about whether his actions please others, but is more concerned about doing what is right, even when it is painful to do so. The person of low integrity will yield to the temptation to feather his own nest at the expense of others.

Handwriting: *clear, open spatial arrangement; no intrusions into middle zone oval letters, moderate regularity, balance of letter forms, good organization.*

Who better than "Honest Abe" to use as an example of integrity. Abraham Lincoln's handwriting is clear and simplified with an excellent balance of space, form, and movement—a good gestalt. The writing flows naturally, without artifice.

Reliability		
Descriptive words:		authenticity, constancy, faithfulness, fidelity, security, steadfastness, trustworthiness.

The reliable person stands by his word, fulfills promises, and finishes what he starts. He has a strong need for closure that makes him most comfortable once decisions have been made. His behavior is consistent and others know they can count on him to be the same tomorrow and next week as he is today. He's not the type to drop a project in the middle and go off on some other tangent.

Handwriting: *moderate regularity, open spatial arrangement, steady baseline, completed lower zone loops.*

Jenny Craig's handwriting below is perfect for both Reliability above and Willpower below. The writing is strong and dynamic, with strong regularity in the middle zone. The zones are overall well-balanced and well-developed. The connective forms are a mixture of curved strokes, which gives her the flexibility to make adjustments as necessary, and straight strokes, which give her willpower and determination, the reliability to get things done.

> *Then set high goals work hard and don't quit until you achieve each one.*

Willpower	
Descriptive words:	discipline, drive, firmness, resolution, self-control, single-mindedness, determination, strength, persistence.

The trait of willpower refers to the strength to act or to refrain from acting. It helps get the job done, whatever the job is, and is connected to goal-directedness. Once the person with strong willpower sets his mind on something, he pursues it with single-minded determination. Willpower is the combination of strength of purpose and a desire for progress, which brings into ideas into reality. It keeps one standing firm in the face of opposition. Of course, in some instances, it takes willpower not to do something.

Handwriting: *regularity, strong t-bars, tight rhythm, some angular forms.*

Initiative vs. Inhibition	
Descriptive words:	(Initiative) self-starter, ambition, drive, dynamism, energy, enterprise, enthusiasm, get-up-and-go, inventiveness, resourcefulness.

Initiative refers to the capacity to get something started without waiting for someone else to take the lead. The person with strong initiative is mentally alert and aware of what needs to be done. He winds himself up and starts working on a project without waiting to be told.

When new or unexpected situations crop up, he literally takes the initiative and responds right away without having to stop and check a rule book or ask someone else for direction.

Handwriting: *(Initiative) simplification, absent initial strokes, fast speed, slightly rising baseline, rightward trend, moderate right slant, horizontal expansion in middle zone, moderate pressure.*

Brad Pitt's writing above is block printing. The simplification, regularity in size, spacing, and baseline (though not perfect, of course), add to the trait of initiative. He's not afraid to move forward and get his needs met.

Inhibition	
Descriptive words:	**(Inhibition): barrier, blockage, in-check, reserve, restraint, reticence, stalling, suppression, curb, control.**

Inhibition is, in many ways, the opposite of initiative. The inhibited person is He is anxious and shy, avoiding social contact as much as possible. He holds back from doing new things or taking the initiative in case he makes a wrong move, takes a wrong step. Intellectually, the inhibited person may be loath to listen to new ideas and concepts, desiring to stay with the familiar and the known as much as possible. Inhibition is present in diagnosed anxiety disorders.

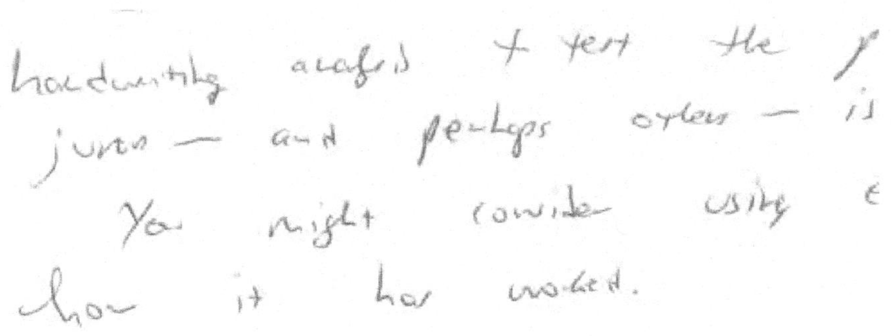

[handwritten text sample]

Handwriting: *(Inhibition): narrow letters, close letter spacing or very wide word spacing, upright or left slant, slower speed, jumpy rhythm, left trend, extra tall upper zone, lack of loops. Changeable slant (insecurity, difficulty making decisions and sticking with them).*

The above writer is a lawyer and the editor of a magazine. The shyness and inhibition he displays is seen in the extremely wide word spacing and jumpy rhythm. His upper zone is tall and the slant is constantly changing.

Below is also an inhibited person, but one who manifests it in a very different way from the previous writer. Notice the narrowness, the angles, and the closeness of the letters. The strong right slant suggests that despite his inhibitions, he feels driven to move towards other people, which can leave him feeling conflicted.

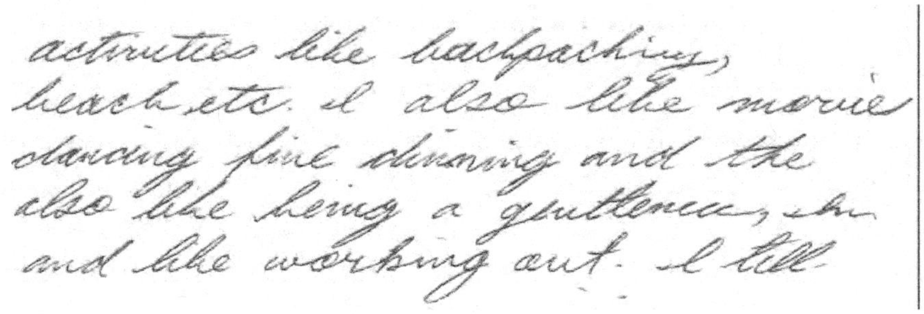

[handwritten text sample]

Conforming vs. Nonconforming	
Descriptive words:	**(Conforming)** accommodating, don't rock the boat, follow the crowd, go by the book, rigid, conventional, average, restrained.

The conforming person is dependent on the approval of others and will bend himself into a pretzel to get that approval. He tends to be pragmatic, practical and realistic. He needs guidelines to follow and is most comfortable sticking to traditional ways of handling problem situations. He believes in a hierarchy where everyone knows their place and sticks within it. It is hard for him to switch horses midstream, and if someone disrupts her emotional equilibrium by acting inappropriately, it takes some effort for him to recover. It is important to note that the conforming person conforms to his/her group, which may not be a conventionally approved group. He might be a gang member, for example, and his behavior conforms to the demands of his social order.

Handwriting: *(Conforming) copybook style, tight rhythm, regularity, narrowness, persona writing style.*

The writing below is the strongly copybook style writing of the conformist (conforming to her chosen social circle).

Conforming vs. Nonconforming		
Descriptive words:		(Nonconforming) independent, flexible, original, creative, daring, unorthodox, weird, freaky, radical, rebel, separatist, oddball, beatnik, bohemian, dissenter, iconoclast, individualist.

The nonconforming person does his own thing and behaves independently of society's rules. He'll break new ground and take on jobs that require expeditious creativity. He doesn't feel threatened by challenge or innovation and will do just about anything as long as it's not part of the old, established methods.

The key is to create a balance between the two extremes of conforming and non-conforming. Actor Robert De Niro's non-conforming personality can be seen in the way he writes in Figure 13 slanted on the page—he does it his own way. The writing is simplified, thready, and written fairly quickly.

Handwriting: (Nonconforming) originality, simplification, balance of curves and angles, narrow right margin, high degree of thready letter forms, pop-up letters, such as the large buckled "k."

Emotional Maturity

Emotional Maturity vs. Hypersensitivity		
Descriptive words:		*(Emotional Maturity) wisdom, well-developed, mellow, sophisticated, completion.*

Emotional maturity might be defined as having developed the ability to control one's intense emotions and behavior, rather than having one's emotions control him. Even under stress, the emotionally mature person will act calmly and wisely. That means living by a set of principles and acting honestly, making good choices even when it's hard.

The emotionally mature person is willing to face the consequences of his actions, accepting and learning from his failures, and keeping a positive mental outlook.

Nobody is perfect, but most of the time the emotionally mature person is able to cope with sudden changes and various stressors. He keeps a reasonable perspective that allows him

18.) At what age are workers considered "through"

19.) How may the occupation be rated as a way of life?

Alex Feller

to maintain an objective position, not getting so caught up in the emotions of the moment that he can't see the big picture.

He deals with his feelings as they occur, rather than repressing them, in an appropriate manner. He knows when it is appropriate to act on his feelings and when to hold back.

> **Handwriting:** *(Emotional Maturity) strong rhythm, simplification, right trend, good organization, clear spatial arrangement, moderate speed, not copybook or persona writing.*

The following handwriting sample was written by the late Felix Klein, one of the great modern graphologists. What he learned during his time spent in German concentration camps during WWII undoubtedly contributed to the emotional maturity seen in his personality, which was reflected in his handwriting.

Emotional Maturity vs. Hypersensitivity		
Descriptive words:		(Hypersensitivity) irritable, nervous, touchy, thin-skinned, emotional, explosive, impatient, unpredictable, volatile.

At the other end of the spectrum of emotional maturity is the hypersensitive person who overreacts, building mountains out of molehills, taking offense wherever he perceives criticism—and he sees criticism everywhere. He finds himself unable to appropriately separate from others, and that has little to do with empathy. Overemotional and reactive, the emotions he expresses tend to be negative ones such as depression and paranoia.

The hypersensitive person is easily swayed and easily hurt. If you express what he perceives to be a negative opinion about his behavior, even though you do it in a kind manner, he feels crushed by it. For him to be able to hear the criticism, you must couch it in compliments.

This type of person continually worries about everything—should I do this or that? Have I made the right decision or choice? Should I do it differently? People who suffer panic attacks are likely to have many of these characteristics.

> **Handwriting:** *(Hypersensitivity) disturbed rhythm, variable middle zone size, variable slant, wavy baseline, changing pressure, enlarged final letter on words, pop-up letters mid-word (acting out), ending strokes that curve back over the final letter (self-protective).*

The handwriting below is Princess Diana's. She was known to be highly sensitive and easily upset, which is seen in the changeable middle zone size in her sample. There are also many positive traits in her handwriting, among which is the excellent spatial arrangement. With good spatial arrangement, the writer is generally able to function well enough to plan and carry out his plans in day-to-day life, even when there are problems in other areas (emotional and/or physical).

Persona		
Descriptive words:		*stiff, assumed identity, not natural, artificial.*

According to C. G. Jung, the persona is the outer display of the personality. It is described as a mask, or several masks, that the writer may wear, depending on the circumstances. Someone may have a particular persona (or face) that they only wear at work, another at home, and another that they show to their friends, depending on the needs of the situation.

The persona writer is afraid to be seen as he or she really is. Deep inside, he's afraid that his true self is unacceptable, so he goes to great lengths to present a facade of what he believes will be "more acceptable."

When the mask becomes so strong that, in effect, it becomes the person (rather than the person simply using the mask), we have a persona handwriting. In that case it becomes necessary to look under the mask to find the true personality.

> **Handwriting:** *The writing may look beautiful but it doesn't look spontaneous. It appears drawn, with an emphasis on appearance, as if it were done for form's sake over function. The way things look are more important to the writer than the content.*

When analyzing persona writing, look beyond the beautiful outer appearance, pay particular attention to word and letter spacing for any little anomalies, such as oddly formed strokes, strokes that go into the lower zone that don't belong there (e.g.: final downstroke on the letter "m" or "h" plunges into the lower zone). There will almost always be some indication of what is behind the mask. This is also true of block printing, which can be a form of persona writing.

The above sample is a persona handwriting with the emphasis on making it beautiful, rather than the message. It looks as if it were drawn, rather than written naturally. Inside, the writer feels that she is lacking, so she wears a beautiful mask so that no one will see who she really is.

Naturalness		
Descriptive words:		*content, happy, poised, peace of mind, relaxed, satisfied, casual.*

Naturalness is the opposite of persona. The natural person behaves spontaneously, free from affectation. He doesn't feel overly constrained by the rules and boundaries of society. Note, however, that it is important for the "natural" person to exercise some self-control so as not to take his naturalness to extremes (in which case he becomes "non-conforming.")

What does "extremes" mean in this case? An example of an extreme would be someone who puts few or no filters on his behavior. Whatever is in his head comes out of his mouth, regardless of whether it is appropriate or not. For example, with a high degree of naturalness, this type might not moderate profanity when there are children or conservative people present. He might tell off-color jokes without regard to his audience. This is part of the inhibitions spectrum.

> **Handwriting:** *free-flowing, loose rhythm, open loops, horizontal expansion, garland forms, lower signs of control (narrowness, tighter rhythm, etc.), medium pressure, medium-fast speed, lack of initial strokes.*

The next sample is written naturally, with an open, loose rhythm. There are few extra strokes, the speed is medium, and it moves to the right without being held back by a lot of elaboration.

Self-Control		
Descriptive words:		**(Positive): disciplined, sober, dignified, discreet, poised, reserved, balance, restraint. (Negative): stoicism, repressed, abstaining, avoidant, self-denial, ascetic, the exercise of restraint, self-command.**

A vital personality trait, Self-control refers to the ability to control or regulate one's emotions and behaviors. It includes appropriate self-denial or putting off satisfying certain needs or desires until a more appropriate time and place. Like all other traits, self-control should be used in moderation because too much self-control can turn into Overcontrol (see below), which is a negative trait.

> **Handwriting:** *strong rhythm, which is along the tighter end of the spectrum (but not too tight), good organization, balanced picture of space, good overall gestalt— the writing doesn't appear too loose or too tight. Well-developed zonal balance (though not too tall or too wide).*

Fiction writer Dean Koontz' writing shows excellent self-control without going into overcontrol. His handwriting stops just short of persona writing, The spacing is a little too compact for the overall size, but there is excellent balance in the zones and firm rhythm.

Thanks for your lovely and very kind letter about Odd Thomas. Sorry to have taken so long to reply, but I was working 90 and more hours a week to finish Velocity and dropped the ball on all correspondence.

Overcontrol		
Descriptive words:		**rigid, unbending, exercising constraint, hold in check, regulating, dominating.**

Overcontrol is the trait of self-control taken to extremes. Underneath is the fear in the overcontrolled person that if he were to allow himself an inch, he would totally lose control and do something outrageous, which would be unacceptable. He needs to know exactly what to expect in a given situation and must have a familiar framework within which to operate. He pressures himself and others with unattainable standards and unrealistic expectations. It's as if a strict parent were constantly looking over his shoulder, scrutinizing everything he does. Is he eating the right food, dressing in appropriate clothes? Toeing the mark?

And likely, it is from growing up with overly strict parenting that this type of person has carried that internal parent with him. As a child he was discouraged (or even intimidated) from expressing negative emotions, such as fear or sadness or anger. Consequently, as an adult he is unable to do so.

Since negative emotions must go somewhere, he turns them inward and they become depression and frustration. The writer is a pressure cooker, and at some point, it is likely and probable that those emotions will explode or he will implode. In either case, the consequences are likely to be negative in the extreme. He may become self-destructive or turn his rage on someone else.

The overcontrolled person might be diagnosed as having Obsessive-Compulsive Personality Disorder.

Handwriting: *overall narrowness, too many angles and retracing, muddy ductus. Overly tall upper zone. Narrow upper zone. Close word spacing, narrow letter spacing, extreme t-crosses.*

The writing below illustrates overcontrol in a woman in her seventies who emphasizes the writing form, taking time to make it attractive. The extreme t-crosses, narrow forms, and retracing tell the real tale of her need to be in control, which is exhibited in subtle, rather than overt ways and with great charm.

Cautious	
Descriptive words:	**(Positive): thoughtful, careful, vigilant, discreet, prudent, watchful. (Negative): calculating, shrewd, playing it cool, political, Machiavellian, cunning, devious, guarded, manipulative, premeditating, wary**

Like most traits, cautiousness can be used for good or bad. Someone who is reasonably cautious is alert in a hazardous situation, paying attention to what is going on around him. An overly cautious person, on the far end of the spectrum tends to be constantly vigilant, always expecting problems, never able to relax. We might even think of him as a bit paranoid. The other side to Cautiousness is the person who is on the lookout for opportunities to scam others. Because he knows he is a scammer or a cheat, he always expects to be cheated by others.

Handwriting: *(Positive): attention to layout, organization, arrangement, which shows ability to plan ahead. (Negative): high degree of secondary thread, thread plus angles, slow speed, very wide word spaces, strong left slant.*

With his narrow letter forms and wide spaces, the next writer shows negative caution to the point of hypervigilance. He is always looking over his shoulder in case someone tries to put something over on him.

The writing below is that of Colleen Barrett, who was president of Southwest Airlines. Her leftward slant and wide word space in a positive gestalt suggest a positive type of cautiousness.

Impulsive	
Descriptive words:	*hasty, imprudent, thoughtless, unguarded, rash.*

The impulsive person tends to be passionate about what he's doing and is easily swayed by emotional impulses. He acts in a spontaneous fashion, rather than thinking before he speaks. This type of person is usually more comfortable speaking extemporaneously on the spur of the moment than taking the time to prepare what he has to say.

Handwriting: *fast speed, strong right slant, rising baseline, narrow margins. Close spatial arrangement, not well organized.*

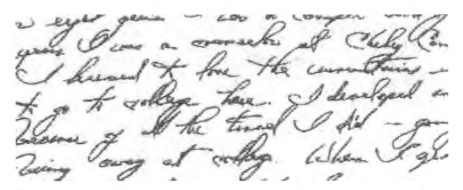

The writer above is extremely impulsive and was accused of some serious crimes, including child molestation. The writing fits all of the descriptive terms.

Calmness		
Descriptive words:		*placid, serene, soothing, serene, tranquil, neutral unruffled.*

The calm person could be described as having a low degree of excitement or passion He remains unperturbed by whatever is going on around him, just letting it all wash over him. This is the type of person who allows others to be who they are and not let it bother him if they aren't just like him.

He's not wound tightly like some types but prefers to go with the flow and count to ten before reacting when a situation becomes tense. This is the person you can go to when you need a listening ear and someone who won't become overemotional about what you're telling them. Think Yoda.

> **Handwriting:** *medium speed, medium pressure, upright loops copybook style, the rhythm has a "soft" look that is almost, but not quite, droopy. Letter forms tend to be garland.*

Mother Teresa's handwriting next is characterized by its large size, garland forms, and steady rhythm.

Dear Canadian Friends,
God love you for all
the love you have shared
with me and the Missio-
caries of Charity and
our Poor throughout

Agitation	
Descriptive words:	*inner commotion, disturbance, turbulence, upheaval, perturbed.*

Have you ever been around someone who can't stop pacing or wringing their hands when they're upsct about something? Those are signs of agitation, which results from inner conflict, anxiety, and highly emotional state. The handwriting analyst will not be able to do determine from just one sample whether agitation is related to a particular situation or is a general state of being for the writer. However, the analyst will certainly detect those qualities as being present.

> **Handwriting:** *jumpy, nervous rhythm, extra-long lower lone, frequent changes of slant, highly variable middle zone height and width, wavy baseline. Sharp tics at the beginnings of letters.*

The handwriting of actor Charlie Sheen, who was allegedly partying with porn stars and using cocaine when he wrote the check below, shows agitation in the extreme variability and changing slant. The rhythm is disturbed.

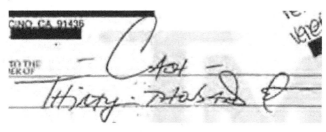

Impassive	
Descriptive words:	Aloof, cool, cold-blooded, inscrutable, indifferent, heartless, dry, composed, phlegmatic, reserved, unemotional

The impassive person acts without emotion, he's unmoved by impassioned appeals. He is cool-minded and his emotions are not easily aroused, so if you need to get through to him, you must do it with logic and reason, not emotion.

Handwriting: *sharp ductus, wide spatial arrangement, upper zone emphasis, narrowness, lack of loops, upright upper zone (no slant), or slight leftward slant.*

Jackie Onassis' handwriting has the reserve and emotional coolness to qualify for the trait of impassiveness. Even before the assassination of her husband, she would not allow herself the freedom to outwardly express her deeper emotions.

I left it open for you to read if you like. Now that I read it the morning after it is much too emotional to send to the poor man — but I just cant write it again

Social Style Spectrum

The way we behave with other people is strongly influenced by our basic temperament, but also by the way our experiences have taught us to respond to our personal environment.

Outgoing (Extraverted)	
Descriptive words:	approachable, extrovert, friendly, genial gregarious, open, sociable, warm, unrestrained, laid-back.

The outgoing person is more concerned with the external environment, things outside the self, rather than interior self-exploration. He's interested in what's going on around him, who's who, and how to connect with them. This person loves to socialize, and if he sees someone he wants to meet, he's not about to sit around waiting for that person to introduce themselves, he'll take the initiative.

When the trait of "Outgoing" gets to be too strong, you have the intrusive person who does not know how to draw appropriate social boundaries.

Handwriting: *medium-large size, right slant, garland forms or mixture of garlands and angles, moderate pressure, right trend, curved initial strokes. Too much outgoingness may be seen in disturbed, jumpy rhythm, showing expenditure of nervous energy, and a crowded picture of space.*

The writing above is a strongly outgoing type with a warm pastose stroke, compact picture of space, strong right slant and speed in strong rhythm.

Loner	
Descriptive words:	isolated, secluded, separate, solitary, solo, introvert, outsider, hermit, lone wolf, individualist, unattached.

A loner is someone who goes beyond simple introversion, to the point of preferring his or her own company over others most of the time. He actively avoids the company of others and is uncomfortable in the presence of more than one or two people. That means he tends to avoid groups as much as possible. He may be shy or he may be an introvert, which simply means that he derives most of his energy from internal, rather than external sources.

Handwriting: *overall wide spatial arrangement, especially extra-wide word spaces, wide line spacing, wide margins, undeveloped lower zone, strong simplification, taller than average upper zone, printed styles, few loops, straight strokes. Simplified lower zone, no wide loops, secondary expansion (narrow letters with wide spaces between them).*

Above is an example of a loner with his left slant and wide word spaces, all of which create a pulling away from other people. The small size and simplified printing show a lack of interest in the outer world.

Demonstrative	
Descriptive words:	**Demonstrative: affectionate, candid, effusive, expansive, outspoken, profuse, unconstrained, unreserved, warmhearted, decisive, emotional, histrionic, gushing.**

One who is demonstrative shows his feelings openly, especially affection. He is outgoing and emotional, having a strong sense of the dramatic. Life is never dull with a demonstrative person around, but he needs someone to play to, and if things are not exciting enough, he's like to do something (demonstrative) to stir things up. His stories are spiced up with colorful details and everything is larger than life. The demonstrative person doesn't simply walk into a room, he makes a grand entrance. He speaks from the heart and there is never any question about his true feelings, as he wears them on his sleeve. This is no shrinking violet; he's warm and flirtatious. A natural performer, he knows how to get the attention he craves.

Taken to extremes, the demonstrative person may be diagnosed with Histrionic Personality Disorder.

Handwriting: *garland forms, few angular forms, pastosity, right slant, close word spacing, medium-wide upper and lower zone loops, possibly a persona style.*

146

We can tell by the large lower loops and close line spacing that the sample[...] is a highly demonstrative person. Interestingly, though, her word spacing is rath[...] she is a converted introvert. That is, she has learned to behave in a more extraverted [...] than is natural to her.

Need for Attention, Affection, Approval	
Descriptive words:	*pleaser, helper, manipulator*

This person is the pleaser who submerges his own needs and wants in order to take care of the needs of others. He will twist himself into a pretzel to be what he thinks others expect him to be, even when that means going against his own basic principles and moral standards. He can't bear criticism because that means he has failed to live up to what the important person in his life wants, and he takes any criticism as rejection.

He expects his important person to provide for him both physically and emotionally, which means he hands that person the power to make him happy or not. He believes that without the love and caring of that person, he would be physically unable to function. When his needs are not met, he is unable to openly express the resentment that he feels, which leads to depression.

This type of person might be diagnosed with Dependent Personality Disorder.

> **Handwriting:** *emphasis on rounded forms, no or few angles, PPI may look like the number 2 or lie on its back. Slack or droopy rhythm, close spatial arrangement, slow-medium speed, smaller capitals.*

Nicole Brown Simpson, whose handwriting appears next, had a strong need for attention, affection, and approval. Her handwriting is extremely rounded (slow arcade and garland letter forms) with virtually no angles to give it strength. The round writing forms are saying

above writer

r large, so

manner

ther than taking care of her own emotional needs, she looked

hese round forms tend to choose abusive men and then
the relationship, begging for the love they need, but can never
out anything to get the approval of their partner.

to see you, to talk to you in
person. But I know you can't do that.
I've been attending these meetings - to
help me turn negatives into positives - to
help me get rid of my anger .... I've
learned to "let things go" (the most

Need to be admired	
Descriptive words:	*self-confidence (too much), pride, self-admiring, egotism, conceited, cocky, hubris.*

While most people enjoy being looked up to and respected when they believe they have accomplished something deserving of respect, the person with the need to be admired goes beyond that point. He thinks he is extra-special and deserves recognition "just because." In his view, his personal qualities are more admirable than others, and he looks down on other people in a condescending, arrogant manner.

He might work hard to do a good job, but his efforts are for the purpose of looking good and outdoing others, rather than for the intrinsic value of the job itself. His need to be admired may include the prestige of owning an expensive car, designer clothing, living in an upscale neighborhood, buying all the latest electronic gadgets. Relationships are selected for how influential they are, even when seeking a mate.

This type might be diagnosed with Narcissistic Personality Disorder.

> **Handwriting:** *strong, tight rhythm, moderate-heavy pressure, large capital letters* (2-3 x mzh), some ornamentation of capitals, underlined signature, not copybook style, well-developed lower zone, right trend, block printed style.

Donald Trump's handwriting has the forceful "look at me" attention-grabbing large capitals of someone who will not be ignored. This writing, which was done around 1991, is all middle-zone block printing. It has not changed a lot in recent years, except that the signature has become tighter and more angular, more aggressive.

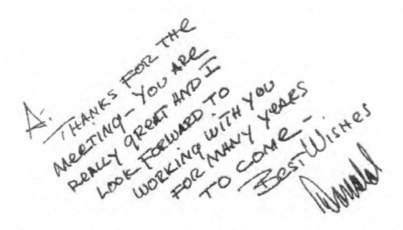

Perfectionist		
Descriptive words:		*stickler, fusspot, idealist, nitpicker, compulsive*

The perfectionist is a high achiever who has gone to extremes. He has a profound need to look smarter, more talented, more knowledgeable, more accomplished than others. He can't stand to be criticized in any way, so he works hard to create an unbreakable mask (persona). If the mask cracks—that is, if he behaves in a manner that does not live up to his carefully constructed image, he feels humiliated, crushed, as if he were nothing.

The perfectionist is also a procrastinator who continues to "put the finishing touches" on a project because if it's not finished, it can't be criticized. He is likely to be self-critical and critical of others, nitpicking tiny imperfections and judging them harshly.

Other traits of perfectionists include the setting of unrealistically high goals. He'll work hard to attain those goals but sets himself up for failure by making them out of reach. When

he fails to meet his goals his mood plunges into despair. A big problem is that the goal means more than the process, so he misses out on a lot of good experiences and feelings.

149

Handwriting: extreme neatness, extreme organization, small overall size, balanced margins, sharp ductus, upright slant, tends to copybook or a persona style. The writing above tends toward copybook, but with some simplification that keeps it in the positive range. There is regularity but also flexibility, neatness, small size, and good organization, with upright slant.

Exploitive		
Descriptive words:		**corrupt, crooked, deceitful, dishonest, mercenary, petty, ruthless, selfish, shameless, underhanded, unethical, unprincipled**

The exploiter sees the world as consisting of two sets of people—those who are weak and those who are strong. He is a user who takes from those who are trusting and kind ("weak" in his eyes), literally using them for his own needs. He will steal from you without conscience, whether what he steals is a romantic partner, an idea, or undercutting you to the boss or your friend behind your back. He sees people as stepping stones to get where he wants to go.

This type is often seen in outside sales positions. Note that there are some who are exploitative but the trait doesn't show up clearly in their handwriting because they have no conscience about their bad behavior. The person who uses his power to exploit others should be considered an aggressor engaging in a destructive form of control.

This person might be diagnosed as Antisocial Personality Disorder or Sociopath.

Handwriting: slack rhythm, extremely heavy or extremely light pressure, heavy cross-outs, muddy ductus, sharp strokes, high degree of angles, double curves, pointed strokes, extremely long, heavy t-crosses, disturbed movement, elliptical form of "g."

Along with his younger brother Erik, Lyle Menendez was convicted of killing their parents. The slack, lazy rhythm and secondary thread forms are the strongest indicators in his writing for the manipulator. In addition, the elliptical form of the "g" on "good" is a strong indicator for this trait.

abused + runaway children is an excellent one. I plan on doing the same thing + Dont lose sight of that goal. The children need it as you know.

Acquisitive	
Descriptive words:	avaricious, close-fisted, grasping, grudging, mercenary, selfish, rapacious, covetous

The acquisitive person wants to acquire and own stuff. He may be greedy, eager to add to his wealth, not in the way of the average person who believes in saving some money for a rainy day, but like the Scrooge who is driven to amass money, things, and sometimes even people, just for the sake of having them.

This is the person for whom the phrase "keeping up with the Joneses" was invented. Spiritual and intellectual pursuits and healthy relationships tend to take a back seat in his life. Having "stuff" makes him feel more secure, yet there can never be enough to satisfy him. The person with many hooks on initial and final strokes lets go of their stuff only with great difficulty. The mere threat of losing ownership of even the smallest of his possessions provokes intense anxiety.

> **Handwriting:** *hooks, especially at the beginnings of letters and words. Large lower zone, large, round middle zone, short upper zone, coiled, rolled strokes.*

[handwriting sample]

The above sample is unusual in its extreme enrolled strokes. The writer is a kleptomaniac. A more common example of the acquisitive person appears next.

She stole money from her employer. Note the long hooks at the beginnings of words. What makes these hooks a red flag is that they are used in combination with slow arcades with an emphasis on the middle zone, which suggests premeditation.

[handwriting sample]

Generosity	
Descriptive words:	*giving, benevolent, altruistic, charitable, hospitable, kind, unselfish, unstinting, philanthropic, noble*

The generous person is ready to give liberally of his resources, be it time, money, or energy, without looking for something in return. He extends what he has willingly and freely. His character is kind and open, free from pettiness. Generosity could be described as "fullness of spirit."

Handwriting: *right trend, garlands, pastosity, strong rhythm, well developed lower zone, pastosity, some extended final strokes, uncluttered oval letters (o, a), horizontal expansion. Lack of overall narrowness.*

The letters in the above writing are narrow (pulling back to self), which takes away from generosity (pulling back to self). However, strong indicators *for* generosity are seen in the long, curved ending strokes that reach out to others, and the general rightward trend.

Adaptability	
Descriptive words:	*ability to make adjustments, flexible, versatile, efficient, resourceful, accommodating, easygoing.*

Adaptability refers to the capacity to make changes as necessary without undue stress. By remaining open to change, the writer allows himself room to adjust to various contingencies. Obstacles that might prove unsurmountable for others are merely molehills to him. When they arise he simply finds the path of least resistance and eases his way over or around the barrier.

He is able to jump easily from one thing to another, handling the more pressing situation, then returning later to finish what he started. This would be harder for a more structured person. He's open to suggestions and usually doesn't mind yielding to the thinking of others where it makes sense.

Handwriting: *some thready forms, garlands, fast arcades, low degree of angles. Forms other than copybook or block printing. Moderate right slant. Fluid letters such as "f" made in one movement. Lack of initial strokes. Lack of strict organization, somewhat disturbed picture of movement, disturbed rhythm.*

Here is a good example of adaptability. The writing is open and expanded, with forms that are flexible and fluid, easy to change direction.

Here's the book as well to thank you & make up the price difference,

Leadership Aptitude	
Descriptive words:	authority, command, control, domination, foresight, initiative, influence, power, drive, intelligence and cognitive abilities, self-confidence, energy, integrity, charisma, assertiveness.

Good leaders have vision—they know where they are going and what it will look like when they get there. They also have to be able to articulate their vision, to share it with their team in a way that will garner enthusiasm and encourage the team to work on their goals together. The good leader can be trusted to maintain his inner values, not speaking from both sides of his mouth, even when it would be easier to do so. He has self-control and doesn't indulge in childish emotional outbursts.

He dedicates himself to the work at hand and keeps moving forward until it is complete. He gives credit where credit is due and takes responsibility for failures. The good leader understands what it means to be humble, not putting himself above others on the team. He listens to new ideas, even though they may not match his current way of thinking and is open to new ways of doing things.

He thinks outside the box, not sticking to old ways just because they've worked in the past. He'll be fair and consistent in the way he treats his subordinates. A good leader will assert himself, stating his expectations clearly and with authority, though not aggressiveness. Above all, a good leader will maintain a sense of humor, keeping a positive mental outlook to help lead his team and keep everyone enthusiastic.

Handwriting: *strong rhythm, medium-strong pressure, well-developed capitals, balanced spatial arrangement, balanced letter forms, especially garlands and angles, well-developed upper zone, simplifications, moderate right trend, high t-crosses.*

There are many different types of leaders, but JFK's writing exemplifies many of the qualities of a good leader. The rhythm is somewhat disturbed, but the rightward trend and the emphasis on the upper zone in the high, flying t-bars indicate that he had a vision for the future and the mental energy to pursue it.

Need for Power and Control, Controlling		
Descriptive words:		Bully, bossy, domineering, pushy, demanding, overpowering

The difference between "Overcontrol" and "Controlling" is that the former refers to exerting tight controls over oneself, while the latter refers more to exerting control over others. Most people need to feel they have a certain amount of power over their own life, but the need for power and control goes above and beyond that degree. Such a person is contemptuous of weakness in himself or others. He expects you to follow his command and believes that his way is always right and nobody else is as competent as he is.

There are many ways of acting out control needs over others. Some are overt, such as giving direct orders and nitpicking, while others are subtler and manipulative. The controlling person believes he always has the answers, for himself and others—it's always "my way or the highway."

Although he seems commanding on the outside, deep inside, he feels insecure and frightened. He has a subconscious fear that if he doesn't control others, they will leave him. The truth is, his controlling manner pushes others away, which turns the fear into a self-fulfilling prophecy.

Handwriting: *narrowness, tall upper zone, high degree of angles, possibly high degree of arcades, t-bars angled down, extremely long t-bars. Tight spatial arrangement.*

Jack Welch, whose handwriting is seen below, was CEO of General Electric. He might not have been hugely popular as a person but he was certainly in control of the company and a very effective manager.

Similar to Donald Trump's writing (which would also fit in this category), it's easy to see the dynamism. The tight spacing allows him to be in control. Welch also has strong rhythm and movement that propels him to the right (the future). It would be very difficult to stand up to someone like this.

Communication Style

Frankness vs. Evasiveness	
Descriptive words:	*aboveboard, artless, blunt, forthright, guileless, outspoken, transparent, truthful, straight, from the hip*

Frankness means putting effort into precisely communicating the relevant material that you want to get across. This is at the other end of the spectrum from the tact and diplomacy. The frank person may blurt out what he is thinking, telling the unvarnished truth. He says it like it is, and you don't have to worry about having to figure out what he meant by what he said.

He values clarity, though that doesn't necessarily mean he'll tell you everything that's on his mind. But at least you'll know that whatever he says is candid and he won't try to spare your feelings. This is not someone whom you should expect to spend a lot of time on small talk.

Handwriting: *(Frank) clear ovals, generally open-looking, lack of initial strokes.*

> THE CORINNE BAILEY RAE CD
> IS VERY MOVING AND WONDERFUL.
> ITS HER FIRST STUDIO RELEASE
> SINCE HER HUSBAND JASON RAE
> DIED OF AN ACCIDENTAL OVERDOSE
> IN 3/08. THERE IS SO MUCH PAIN

The above writer is frank and open in the way she communicates. She pulls no punches and says exactly what she thinks, regardless of time or place. The all-middle zone block printing is clear and open, with wide word spaces, which indicate that she demands her own space.

Evasive	
Descriptive words:	*ambiguous, cagey, cunning, deceptive, devious, elusive, indirect, lying, misleading, oblique, unclear, vague.*

The evasive person communicates in such a way that it's hard to make sense of what he's said. He keeps things ambiguous so that when you come back later and quote him, he can respond, "but that's not what I meant." He may tell lies, or just bend the truth until it squeals.

He'll say what he thinks others want to hear, maneuvering around the facts and avoiding by indirection or misdirection. He may not even mean to be misleading, he may just want to make the other person happy, so makes it sound as if he has the answers to all of their problems. What he doesn't say, or what he doesn't talk about is another matter altogether.

Handwriting: *(Evasive) double-looped ovals, stabbing strokes or other "junk" in oval letters, secondary thread forms, variability in size, slant, baseline, form.*

> let me start this letter off
>) thank you nija for the sta
>) sent me " that was really
> and I think that was real

The evasiveness in the above writing is seen in the combination of left slant and wide word spaces. There is also real pathology in the ovals that are open at the bottom. He will never, ever tell the truth. The writer is a gang member who spent substantial time in prison for violent offenses.

Argumentative	
Descriptive words:	belligerent, bellicose, truculent, contrary, irritable, touchy, hostile, combative, contentious, contrary, controversial, factious, opinionated, touchy, carping, demanding.

The argumentative person is quick to take offense. He enjoys debate for its own sake and may see life as a game where he must always stay one-up. Insisting on explaining his point to the nth degree, the writer sees himself as simply being thorough and complete. Others, however, see him as argumentative.

He feels a strong need to defend his ideas and actions, so it seems as if he is always tense and ready to fight. This is the person whose chin is stuck out, lips pursed, hands gripped in a tight fist. He's willing to go over and over a point to make sure his message is getting across. Even when the other person would rather change the subject, the argumentative person keeps pushing until his opponent is beaten and gives up or becomes convinced of his point of view.

Handwriting: *high degree of angular forms, sharp strokes tall upstroke on "p,"* tight rhythm, high degree of connectedness.

The handwriting above has many angles and sharp strokes and highly connected. The tall downstroke on the "p" and an extra tall upper zone that points to authoritarianism adds to the picture of argumentativeness.

Persuasive		
Descriptive words:		enticing, forceful, impressive, moving, seductive, slick, smooth, authentic, convincing, plausible.

Unlike the argumentative person, the persuasive one is able to get his point across without offending his listener. He makes the other person feel as if he understands and relates to them on their own level, and he does this by establishing rapport with them.

Good intuition is probably part of the ability to persuade. A really persuasive person can be quite articulate and has the capacity to move an audience to tears with just a few well-chosen words.

> **Handwriting:** *primary thread with garland forms, light-moderate pressure, looser rhythm, moderate-fast speed, slight right slant, baseline not too firm, but rising, some smooth breaks, but mostly connected.*

President Barack Obama (above) is well known for his persuasive oratory. In the sample below he uses garland forms with some thread, a bouncy rhythm, and the writing has a few smooth breaks.

Sandy—

THE WHITE HOUSE
WASHINGTON

Thanks for the wonderful and thoughtful letter. It is because of outstanding Americans like you that I committed to changing our current policy. Although it will take some time to complete (partly because it needs Congressional action) I intend to fulfill my commitment!

Tact & Diplomacy		
Descriptive words:		artfulness, delicacy, discretion, poise, discernment, shrewdness, subtlety.

By softening harsh words with delicacy, the tactful person is adept at handling the feelings of others. This is not someone domineering or demanding, but one who elicits cooperation kindly and with charm. He can deliver unpleasant news with the diplomacy of a Henry Kissinger, defusing tense situations with aplomb, no matter how stressful the situation may be.

> **Handwriting:** *similar to Persuasiveness, primary thread with garland forms, light-moderate pressure, looser rhythm, moderate-fast speed, slight right slant, no sharp or pointed strokes.*

President Bill Clinton is well known for his tact and diplomacy, and we see signs of it here in his left-slanted, garland-heavy writing.

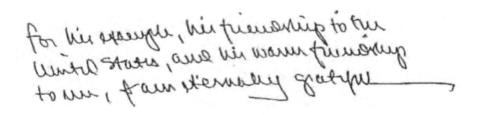

Sensitive		
Descriptive words:		susceptible, discerning, "street smarts," native intelligence, intuitive

Sensitive can mean many things, but in this context, we refer to the ability to react to stimuli, external or internal. This is related to intuition and means the writer picks up on (or is sensitive to) what's going on around him without having to first listen to a lengthy explanation. There is a Sensitive Personality Disorder, in which the person needs a high degree of routine in his life. He cares deeply about what others are thinking about him, and he doesn't make snap judgements. That is not what we're talking about in this case.

> **Handwriting:** *some variability in middle zone size, good distribution of all four connective forms, smooth breaks within words, rhythm may be somewhat disturbed. Open, airy spatial arrangement, light-medium pressure, simplification of form, originality.*

Actor Martin Sheen's writing has a sensitive quality in the openness and right trend. Yet, in his signature the long, straight final stroke says he holds others at arm's length. The Interesting "Th" combination in "Thanks" tells us that he's a quick thinker who is able to rapidly pick up what's going on around him.

Manipulative		
Descriptive words:		*Machiavellian, artful, canny, cautious, circumspect, guarded, cunning, crafty, shrewd, sharp, sly, devious*

The manipulator is a chameleon who has the ability to adopt any behavior or role that serves his purposes. He appears to be accommodating and considerate of your viewpoint and requirements; he seems to be a people-person, but in truth, there is an underlying insistence on having things his own way. All of a sudden you are confronted with an attitude that he's got to have it his way. His idea of compromise is to get part of what he wants now and the rest later. This is someone who deals sweetly with you, but later you'll realize you had the ground cut right out from under you.

Everything he does is self-oriented. He is always calculating the odds and the costs, maneuvering the situation around to suit his own needs. Certainly, he is a charmer when he believes there is a good reason to exert his charm. He knows how to capitalize on the strengths of others and turn things to his advantage. The irony is, when the manipulator believes he's been manipulated, he is outraged.

> **Handwriting:** *high degree of secondary thread forms or combined thread and angles; slack rhythm, high degree of variability in size, slant, baseline, and form.*

I am Proposing that True and Lillie to with me, as they always have. I'm proposing three weeks with me and I send then back to . . . until

The slack rhythm allows the above writer to manipulate her way to getting what she wants. With the large hooks in the upper zone, she can smile to your face while using the open hooks in the lower zone to pick up something behind your back. The large letters mid-sentence become like inappropriate capitals, which suggest that the writer acts out suddenly and emotionally. She will find a way to achieve her aim.

Sense of Humor		
Descriptive words:		*high spirits, lightness, whimsy, wit, fun.*

There are many types of humor, but in general, one with a positive sense of humor is able to defuse difficult situations and bring one through potential disasters virtually unscathed. The person with the sense of humor is able to get through tough times when things are going poorly.

Good humor helps one see the lighter side of things, and good timing is an important part of it. The ability to laugh with others and at oneself helps keep one from becoming rigid and too serious. This trait goes hand in hand with optimism and helps release tension.

Humor can be used as the balm to keep the wheels of relationships running smoothly. The important thing is not to allow humor to devolve into cutting or hurtful sarcasm.

Handwriting: *bouncy rhythm, combination of letter forms, smooth breaks between letters, moderate right trend, some wavy strokes in the upper zone.*

The next handwriting is late comedian Robin Williams'. The lively right trend with large writing and a loose rhythm in the larger writing reveals his ability to jump around with the flexibility needed in his craft. Like Donald Trump and Robert DeNiro, he chose to write at an extreme slant, showing an insistence on doing things his own way, going against the grain of society.

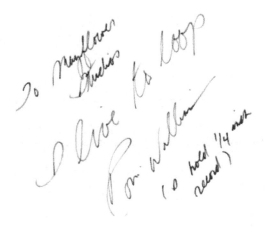

Intellectual Style

Logical		
Descriptive words:		cogent, coherent, discerning, judicious, sensible, sound

Everything this person says can be backed up by data and facts. He notices right away when someone makes a statement that is inaccurate or contradictory and finds it hard to tolerate those who communicate in a way that is less than clear. He wants to know that there is a sound reason for everything he does. He processes his feelings through his intellect. He takes a step by step approach to solving problems. It makes him feel uncomfortable when he's forced to jump into new areas without having time to carefully plan out the next step.

> **Handwriting:** *high degree of connectedness, rounded tops on "m" and "n," combination of connective forms.*

Albert Einstein's handwriting has the strong degree of connectedness of one who reasons things out, rather than feeling them. This is not to say he was an unfeeling person—not at all. There is right slant, which expresses feelings.

163

Analytical		
Descriptive words:		detailed, diagnostic, dissecting, inquisitive, perceptive, questioning, systematic, testing

The analytical person carefully analyzes the whys and wherefores of everything, digging for the facts before reaching a conclusion. He constantly evaluates everything, taking a concept or idea apart piece by piece before accepting it. He's a born skeptic who questions and demands proof.

Handwriting: *high degree of angles, especially in "m" and "n", dashed or tent i-dots.*

Author Malcolm Gladwell's sharp, angular handwriting reveals his analytical, questioning nature. He digs incessantly for the reasons why, never satisfied with the answers he gets.

Attention to Details		
Descriptive words:		analytical, focused, follow-through, diagnostic, inquisitive, penetrating, precise, critical thinker, correct, scrupulous, meticulous, careful, uncompromising, exact

One who pays close attention to details is the one who makes and sticks to a budget, balances his checkbook every month, and knows where everything is on his desk, even if it's messy. He may make lists, checking off items as they are completed, and in the meantime follows procedures step-by-step, making sure that everything is done that needs to be. Routine tasks are approached with care and this person can be expected to complete his tasks thoroughly and completely.

Handwriting: *diacritics* carefully placed (i.e., small round i dots, careful *t-crossings), good overall organization, regularity, copybook style, legibility, medium speed.*

The above writing illustrates someone who pays very close attention to details. See the careful, round dots over the "i's"? Every letter is carefully made, though not to an extreme, so it's still interpreted positively. The spacing is slightly to the weak end of the spectrum but again, not extreme.

Intuitive	
Descriptive words:	*innate, spontaneous, perceptive, visceral, canny, ingenious, insightful, perspicacious, sensitive*

The intuitive person is quick to grasp the bottom line. He "gets" information without stopping to thinking about it and is able to listen for the gist of a matter, skimming the surface to pick up what he needs to know and discarding the rest. This allows him to sum up people and situations quickly and easily.

His uncanny intuitive sense tells him the mood of a room from the moment he walks in. He doesn't need to hear the whole story, but is miles ahead, already figuring out how new information will fit in with what he already knows and how to use it.

As if scanning the environment with an invisible antenna, he picks up anything that might be helpful and discards the rest. He's learned that he can skim the surface and trust his gut instincts. He tends to work in bursts of energy, following his inspiration where it leads him.

165

Handwriting: *light-medium pressure, simplification, disturbed rhythm, fast arcade forms in the upper zone, open spatial arrangement, smooth breaks between letters (abrupt breaks between letters are more related to one who jumps to conclusions—perhaps the wrong conclusion).*

The next writer is a professional psychic. His high level of intuition is seen in the flat, openness of his writing, which allows information to come to him from above and from below. The writing is mostly connected, with a few breaks at the beginnings of words. The rhythm is jumpy and loose, which is often (but not always) the case with highly intuitive writers.

Imagination		
Descriptive words:		*creative thought, enterprise, fantasy, ideas, imagery, invention, originality, vision, conception*

Imagination is the ability to form mental images of ideas or concepts that are not perceived in reality. This trait allows one to experience worlds of his own creation, looking at things from various points of view and exploring other realms.

Imagination may occur while one is daydreaming, while the conscious mind is actively engaged elsewhere. The question becomes one of whether the daydreamer just "woolgathers," or puts his daydreams to some practical use.

Imagination helps us think outside the box, finding new solutions to old problems.

Handwriting: *well-developed upper zone, some elaboration of capital letters, originality of form, pastosity.*

Probably no one is better known for their imagination than Walt Disney. Yet, there's nothing really special about his handwriting.

This is a good lesson for all of us to let the handwriting tell us about the person, rather than projecting our own feelings about what the writing "should" say. The most important facet of Disney's writing is the openness and loose rhythm. His mind was open to new ideas and whatever his intuition brought him.

Idiosyncratic Thinking		
Descriptive words:		distinctive, peculiar, quirky, individualistic, singular, special

Idiosyncratic may refer to a whole range of behaviors, from what is particular to an individual, to one who has his own world view and sees things differently from the rest of us. He behaves in ways that others consider odd or quirky, and they may see him as "peculiar" or "different." This trait may encompass the gifted mentally ill or the brilliant but eccentric genius. At the extreme end of the spectrum, the idiosyncratic thinker might be diagnosed with Schizoid Personality Disorder.

Handwriting: *unusual upper zone, including twisted upper loops and/or extreme height and width, extreme simplification.*

The following sample reveals one who lives in his own world. The extreme narrowness combined with wide spaces suggests paranoia.

167

the function of art to express the truth and it in what sense:
we use literature to convince the reader of the tr
we use literature to establish   some sense the tru
sense if any is it the object of fiction to med.
does life should mean by artistic plausibility

Optimist vs. Pessimist		
Descriptive words:		*(optimist) positive, hoper, idealist, enthusiast, escapist, romantic*

Here we have the question, "is the glass half full or half empty?" The optimist sees the possibilities in life and believes he has the personal power to change what he doesn't like and make of the situation what he wants. He takes responsibility for his life and doesn't try to place the blame for negative events on others. When things go right he expects them to continue going right. When things go wrong, he sees it as a one-time fluke.

Handwriting: *(optimist) slight rising baseline, fairly steady baseline, right slant, moderately loose rhythm, horizontal expansion, moderate pressure.*

The writer's optimism is obvious in the open, fun-loving appearance and slight uphill baseline. A baseline with an exaggerated uphill slant is more often someone who is working at being optimistic but who is actually fighting depression. Here, we have the genuine thing. This young woman in her mid-twenties has a happy spirit and is ready to try anything.

why am I doing this
handwriting analysis thing?
Just for the fun of it all.
What does it all mean?

Pessimist		
Descriptive words:		(pessimist) complainer, cynic, defeatist, depreciator, downer, gloomy, killjoy, wet blanket

The pessimist has the opposite world view. When something goes wrong, he believes that more things are going to go wrong and that he has no control over his life. When something goes right, he figures that was a lucky fluke that isn't going to happen again. Research shows that optimists live longer and have happier, more fulfilled lives.

Handwriting: *(pessimist) narrowness, falling baseline, extreme pressure (light or heavy), cramped appearance.*

The writing above slants downhill. There is virtually no energy behind the pen. This person is not just depressed, he has a generally negative mental outlook and it is almost impossible at this point for him to pull himself up out of the "slough of despond."

Objectivity vs. Subjectivity		
Descriptive words:		(objectivity) detached, dispassionate, equality, open-minded, cool, neutral, even-handed, nonpartisan, unprejudiced

The objective person is able to look at all sides of an issue and view it from an unemotional stance, remaining neutral. He is able to stand back and view the big picture without being unduly influenced by personal feelings or interpretations. He maintains an unbiased stance.

There is such a thing as becoming too objective, where the person disallows any emotional input at all, which may be just as bad as being too subjective.

Handwriting: *(objectivity) generally open spatial arrangement, lack of rigidity, low degree of angles, some variation in slant, word spaces slightly wider than average, simplification, low degree of upper zone loops, some thread, sharp ductus.*

Primatologist Jane Goodall's writing has an open, airy spatial arrangement which, along with the mostly upright slant, provide the perspective to see all sides of a situation before

> For Sheila Lowe –
> I feel quite nervous to inscribe this book for you – it will say so much more to you than to anyone else! Thank you so much for your analysis. And for involving the others.
>
> Jane Goodall

acting. The writing is simplified to its bare bones, with the emphasis on the message, not the appearance. In addition, the wide word spaces and lack of loops indicate an independent thinker who is quite far along the objectivity spectrum. She may have many fluctuating feelings (changing slant, size), but she also has the ability to step back from her emotions and consider them rationally.

Subjectivity	
Descriptive words:	*(subjectivity) biased, personal, biased, arbitrary, attached, egotistical*

The subjective person becomes emotionally overinvolved and so close to a situation that he is unable to detach from it and view it clearly. He sees only how the ma matter affects him, rather than looking at the whole picture and places too much emphasis on his own moods, attitudes, and opinions.

Handwriting: *(subjectivity) crowded spatial arrangement, narrow word spacing, wide loops, larger than average size, narrow margins, rounded letter forms, slow arcades, garlands, pastosity.*

Below is a highly intelligent, rapid thinker, but the writing is so crammed together that he leaves no room for objectivity. He finds it difficult to acknowledge the thoughts and feelings of others. This sample would also be a good candidate for the trait of Argumentative with all its sharp strokes and angles. The writing is too narrow in proportion to the middle zone height.

Openness to Change vs. Closed-mindedness Spectrum	
Descriptive words:	*(openness) accepting, approachable, broad-minded, tolerant, progressive*

Openness to change suggests someone who is ready to try new activities and new methods of accomplishing the same old tasks. A high degree of this trait is closely associated with a good self-image and strong ego. If the degree of openness is too great, the writer may be ready to change on a dime, or he may need a little prep time to deal with major changes. There are several different dimensions for change that can be examined: affective (feeling), cognitive (thinking), and behavioral (acting).

Handwriting: *width of loops, simplification, speed, open spatial arrangement, rhythm on the looser side of the spectrum.*

The writer below may be open-minded (see the wide-open loops and generally loose rhythm), but the changeable slant indicates someone who goes to the extreme and switches side with the wind. So, he may be willing to listen to your great new idea, but that doesn't mean he won't be listening to someone else's five minutes later. He is at the extreme end of the open-mindedness spectrum.

[handwriting sample]

Closed-minded		
Descriptive words:		(closed) inflexible, obstinate, pigheaded, rigid, dogmatic, hidebound, intolerant, opinionated, partisan

A closed-minded person is satisfied that the way they do things is the only way to do them. Those with a poor ego are more likely to stick to what they know and refuse to be open to new things. Low job satisfaction has also been identified with those who are not open to change.

> **Handwriting:** _narrow loops or retraced upper loops, copybook style, lack of simplification, slower speed, cramped spatial arrangement, overly tall upper zone, rhythm on the tighter side of the spectrum._

The next writer is an authoritarian, highly religious individual who is satisfied with what he already knows and has zero interest in opening up to any new ideas. The lower zone is stunted, too, so the energy he uses is mostly intellectual, rather than expended in actually getting things done. He's the type who studies the bus schedule so closely that he misses the bus.

[handwriting sample]

Note the extremely tall, retraced upper zone letters, which signifies his closed-mindedness. The extreme upper zone height is symbolic of reaching up to the heavens, which is more apt to be found in the writing of religious, rather than spiritual people—and there can be a big difference. This phenomenon is frequently found in those who are strongly attached to organized religion.

Energy Level

Vitality	
Descriptive words:	animation, intensity, get-up-and-go, vivaciousness, sparkle, stamina, zest, vigor, exuberance

Vitality refers to physical or mental strength, the capacity to move, to develop and grow. Someone with vitality is able to get a lot done and has a special ability to enjoy life and be productive.

Handwriting: *strong rhythm, moderate-heavy pressure, moderate right trend. Tall capitals. Good zonal balance. The writing looks energetic, strong, as if it's going somewhere (forward).*

The strong vitality in the above writing can be seen in the dark, colorful writing and rightward trend. At the same time, the writing is very narrow, which suggests a conflict. This is a case of driving with one foot on the gas and the other on the brakes. When we learn that the writer is elderly, that makes sense. She is still enthusiastic about life but is at a point where she's facing her own mortality, which brings some concern about the future (therefore, narrowness, holding back).

Enthusiasm		
Descriptive words:		intense interest in a pursuit, energy expended towards a goal. Ardor, eagerness, passion, joie de vivre, possible: spirit of adventure

Enthusiasm is the lively interest in an activity or idea and is often seen in tandem with vitality. Like the old commercial, this person's motto might be, "you only go around once in life," and he's determined to grab every experience he can. Because he lives so much in the moment, it is important for him to remember to stop and smell the roses, rather than dashing from one thing to another without savoring anything (which would be toward the extreme end of the Enthusiasm spectrum).

Handwriting: *strong right trend, elastic rhythm, some angles mixed with garlands and thread. Medium to larger overall size, well-developed lower zone, high flying i dots. Medium to slightly heavy pressure, fast speed, slightly rising baseline.*

This writing is bursting with enthusiasm despite the narrowness. You can "feel" the writing moving forward towards the right.

Lethargy		
Descriptive words:		listless, dull, lacking energy, indifferent, lazy, apathetic, disinterest, dullness, impassivity, sleepiness, laziness, depression, apathy, torpid

Lethargy is the opposite of vitality. The lethargic person just doesn't have the energy to bother. He's the couch potato or constant video game player who rarely gets out of his chair. Taking a walk or doing anything active doesn't appeal to him. There may be physiological issues such as disturbances in blood sugar or circulation, or the culprit might be depression. These should be ruled out with a checkup before concluding that lethargy is a personality trait.

Handwriting: *slack or droopy rhythm, light pressure, left trend, falling baseline. Lethargy suggests tiredness, boredom, depression perhaps. The writer can hardly lift his hand to move the pen along the paper, let alone get anything done.*

Vitality and Activity (next) may seem the same, and they are related, but the difference is, vitality is the writer's basic life force or drive that is available to the personality, while activity refers to the use to which that drive is put.

the project had to be postponed because the geese which went to supply the quills had been stolen. Imagine the anger caused by the untimely theft. Is this story true, or just a tall tale? Your guess is as good as mine.

The writing above has the droopy rhythm of someone who is depressed and just can't get himself going. Depression is often caused by anger turned inward against the self. There is also likely to be a physiological issue with this writer considering the shaky strokes throughout.

Activity		
Descriptive words:		*Liveliness, hardworking, movement, active, enterprising, exertion, animation, liveliness.*

Activity generally refers to the state of being active or busy with the challenges of daily life. However, there is more than one kind of activity: the activity of a busy, well-organized person who gets a lot done, and the frenetic activity of one who just needs to be moving all the time, but not much gets accomplished. The handwriting indicators will be quite different for each.

Handwriting: *(Positive): clear spatial arrangement, good organization on the page, balanced margins, developed lower zone.*

The energy is strong and directed. The picture of space is weak because it is crowded, but along the activity spectrum, this writer is a hard worker who gets a lot done.

[Handwriting sample in cursive script]

Handwriting: *Negative: crowded spatial arrangement, zonal interference (loops written over, the right margin runs off the edge of the page, or the writer writes in the margins, sideways). You will see from the appearance of the writing that the writer feels compelled to stay busy and always has plenty going on.*

The activity in the next sample (next) is frenetic. His energy flies all over the place, as seen in the high degree of variability in size, slant, and form. The rhythm is disturbed.

[Handwriting sample: "Found not guilty - but not Innocent. There is a higher court..." with signature]

Inertia	
Descriptive words:	immobility, listlessness, sluggishness, unresponsiveness, inactivity, slow, smoldering, sluggishness, at rest

Inertia is similar to apathy but is not quite as far along the spectrum. Someone who is apathetic doesn't give a damn. With inertia, the writer just needs a push to get going. Think of a car with a starter problem. If you get behind it and give it a push, the starter engages and the car will keep moving until you deliberately bring it to a stop. The person who suffers from inertia may be fine once he's had a boost. Felix Klein used to say that this type needed an extra cup of coffee in the morning to get himself going.

Handwriting: *speed, either light pressure or very heavy pressure. Overly rounded letter forms, long lead-in strokes, droopy rhythm, slow arcades. Left trend. Wide right margin and/or narrow left margin. The baseline may be concave, sagging in the middle, then returning to a more standard movement.*

The next writer under "inertia" is an underachiever. There is some intelligence in the connection of "o" to "f" in "of." However, the writing movement is weak, showing a of left trend in the many strokes that pull to the left ("r" in "present") and "o" in "emotions."

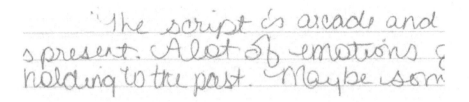

Apathy	
Descriptive words:	*blah, emotionally cool or even cold, flat affect, impassive, indifferent, overly laid back, unresponsive, "what the hell" attitude*

In the apathetic person there is an absence of passion or emotion, a lack of excitement; in fact, a lack of interest in much of anything. Apathy may be an indicator for depression, or the person may be far along the schizotypal spectrum (not to be confused with schizophrenic), which is an affective disorder.

The apathetic person isn't much concerned with life beyond the basics; he seems indifferent and unresponsive. It's a case where "the flesh is willing but the spirit is weak." He is not moved by much and remains impassive an unemotional in most situations. There is a blunting of the emotions, which may have been brought on by traumatic events.

Handwriting: *lack of dynamism, short t-bars, light i dots, droopy rhythm, falling baseline. Sagging garlands, lack of angles, falling baseline. The writing looks like the writer just can't be bothered to put any oomph into it. It just sits there on the page.*

The writer below is highly intelligent but puts little energy into anything he does, except when he suddenly wants something (long t-crosses), in which case he can suddenly become a whirlwind of activity.

desperately need two lecturers, one full time and one part time. Lecturing will be to ...

Goal-directed	
Descriptive words:	industrious, inspired, resourceful, self-starter, striving, assertive, driven, eager, earnest, patient

The goal-directed person is driven to get going and finish what he starts, devoting himself to his work, blocking out distractions until he has accomplished what he set out to do. When barriers arise to his objectives, he finds ways over, around, or through them and continues on his way. His focus is less on immediate gains and more on the future, so he's capable of intense, single-minded effort and knows how to plan ahead and get where he wants to go.

> **Handwriting:** *right trend, long t-bars, t-bars crossed 2/3 or higher on the stem, medium-strong pressure, narrowing right margin, strong rhythm, long, full lower zone, completed lower zone upstrokes, regularity, lack of initial strokes.*

John D. Rockefeller's writing is nothing if not goal-directed. Even though the overall writing is quite small, it covers a lot of ground, with very long t-crosses and rightward movement. He never stops until he reaches his goal, and if that means steamrollering anyone who gets in the way, so be it.

Serial Killers
The Face of Evil

By Sheila Lowe

© 1993 by Sheila R. Lowe

Updated 2011

All rights reserved. No portion of this book may be reproduced, by any process or technique, without the express written consent of the author, except small excerpts, for purpose of review.

Serial Killers - The Face of Evil

He was handsome, charismatic, captivating, and he was convicted of murdering ten women in Florida. Like many other serial murderers, Robert Joseph Long fit right into society, appearing enough like everyone else that he was able to elude capture for many months, all the while raping and killing.

The FBI has a difficult time creating a profile of the typical serial killer because they look just like *us*. To qualify for the FBI definition of a serial killer, an individual must "kill at least three times, with a cooling off period in between." The cooling off period may be as short as a few hours, or as much as several years.

Serial killing is by no means a new phenomenon. In fact, the worst offender may have been Elizabeth Bathory, who lived in the 1600's. Bathory was convicted of killing 650 young women so she could bathe in their blood.

Closer to modern times, we all know about Jack the Ripper, who terrorized prostitutes in Victorian England, where he butchered several women in the late 1800's. There have been several fascinating television programs and books speculating about the various suspects, who even included the grandson of the Queen of England, but his true identity remains a mystery, at least to the general public. The handwriting of the most likely one appears later in this paper.

The demographics of serial murderers indicate that the most likely candidates—85% of convictions—are white males, 20-30 years old. Only 8% of convicted serial killers are women, 15% are black, and 2.5% Hispanic. There are only two cases on record where the killer is, in one instance an Oriental, and in another, an American Indian. North America has the lead in this crime, with 76% of the victims. Europe comes in second at 19% and communist countries have reported only 10 cases since 1917. Eighteen percent of cases remain unsolved.

Just as other violent crimes are on the increase, so is serial murder. In the last 100 years 457 offenders apprehended killed 1300 victims. Between 1900-1950, police recorded an average of only 1.2 cases of serial murder a year. In 1960 there were 12 cases a year. By the 1980's, this offense had jumped to an alarming average of two cases a *month!* Since 1977 one hundred-ninety-one serial killers have been convicted, with 1007 victims. Your pocket calculator will quickly tell you that this means that 77% of serial murders have occurred in less than 20 years.

In an attempt to deal with this escalating problem, the FBI has developed a computerized system of tracking criminals called VICAP, an acronym for Violent Criminal Apprehension Program. This immense data base of information allows police departments across the country to match similar patterns of activity.

When a crime is committed, participating police departments complete a detailed questionnaire about the crime. The information is entered into the computer and cross-matched, so that any similar activities are highlighted. Thus, a criminal like Ted Bundy, who raped and murdered his way across the United States might be apprehended through coinciding modus operandi.

VICAP has faced challenges, partly due to a lack of cooperation by various police departments. In high profile crimes, egos may get in the way, and due to concern for losing the credit for capturing a high-profile killer, the details of these crimes become a closely guarded secret. Also, some smaller police departments may not be equipped with the sophisticated computer equipment required, which limits VICAP's effectiveness.

What makes a serial killer?

Dr. Ken Magid discusses the "Bonding Cycle" in his disturbing book, *High Risk—Children Without A Conscience*. This cycle is made up of 1. An infant's needs, 2. Its rage reaction to the need, 3. Gratification or relief, and 4. Trust when the need is met. The infant's interactions with its mother are what teach it about life and other people.

Right from the start, a baby begins to respond to the sound of its mother's voice and the touch of her hands. If those experiences are harsh and jarring, the damage can be profound. If the baby is not handled with love or, worse, not handled at all, it does not learn how to relate to other human beings. Babies need to have eye contact with other people and they need to be touched.

According to a study by Dr. Ruth Rice, babies that were massaged daily for four months were more advanced neurologically, psychologically and physiologically than other babies.

A baby's physical needs, including feeding may be met, but other important needs may be neglected, such as ignoring its cries for attention. It was found that men who grew up to be serial killers had often been fretful or hyperactive babies, which undoubtedly exacerbated their already abusive or neglectful mothers' emotional abandonment. After all, isn't it easier to love a happy, smiling baby than a constantly crying one?

So, even before they learned to verbalize them, these children discovered that getting their needs satisfied was a losing proposition. At this point, the important bonding between child and others (first, his mother or other primary caregiver) is broken. In effect, the child subconsciously decides, "I'll never let myself be in this painful position again. I'm going to do to others before they can do to me."

Robert Ressler, the former FBI agent who developed a profile of the serial killer, interviewed a large number of convicted serial murderers. He found that without exception, these people had fantasized about murder from childhood and adolescence. Just as motivational speakers teach us to visualize in our mind's eye our desired goal every day in order to make it a reality, these killers visualized torture and murder until it became so real in their minds that carrying out their fantasies became the natural thing to do.

Unable to sustain normal relationships with other people, they fantasized themselves as the aggressor to compensate for their early abuse. Most normal people have fantasies, but these people go far beyond the norm, imagining inexpressible horrors and believing themselves invincible in carrying them out. Not satisfied within normal relationships and activities, they create sexually violent fantasies in a world that they can control. And once they begin on their evil journey, killing becomes an all-consuming obsession, therapy is useless.

Interestingly, an over-protective mother can have just as negative an effect on her child as a neglectful mother. By constantly anticipating the baby's needs before he has a chance to experience them she deprives him of the ability to learn healthy responses to frustration. Additionally, when no limits are set on a child's behavior, he has no way of learning to distinguish right from wrong.

Ressler notes that, "The children who grow up to murder never truly comprehend the world in other than egocentric terms, because their teachers—principally their mothers—do not train them properly in this important matter."

According to Ken Magid a child acquires 50% of his lifetime knowledge within the first year of life and 75% by the end of the second. Therefore, his first experiences will have a profound effect on the rest of its life. If the infant does not make the attachment to its mother, or if the bonding is broken and not re-formed, severe damage *will result*. Furthermore, Magid opines, beyond the age of 12 it is virtually impossible to re-establish that bond.

The childhood home of the serial killer

It has long been accepted that the symptoms of serial murder begin developing in early childhood with a cluster of characteristics that include arson, bedwetting, and cruelty to animals. It has been documented that half the children who engage in these three antisocial behaviors will continue them into adulthood, with the rest experiencing other types of serious psychological problems. Outwardly, their homes may have appeared normal, but they were in fact dysfunctional. The relationships of these children to their mothers were invariably cool and distant.

These children are likely to grow up in homes where their parents don't get along or the father is absent. Poverty or social disadvantages *may* play a part. While in some cases there are physiological components such as schizophrenia, which may aggravate the development of the serial killer mentality, severe child abuse is virtually always a key factor. Discipline is extremely harsh or perhaps worse, inconsistent.

Inconsistent discipline puts the child in a double bind. A parent who allows a particular behavior in one set of circumstances but not when a similar set or circumstances arise, leaves him confused, not knowing what to expect.

Several serial killers reported being forced to wear girls' clothing as punishment. The resulting gender confusion only added to their feelings of frustration, futility, and isolation.

A major characteristic of the serial killer's personality is an inability to maintain a truly loving relationship with another person. The lack of touching and emotional warmth from their mothers prevented them from learning early on how to cherish other humans or how to show affection. Often subjected to extremely stressful sexual events, including molestation and incest, many of them were forced to attend, watch, or participate in their mothers' sexual activities.

By the age of 12 the most important aspects of psychological makeup are entrenched. With the onset of adolescence, these children of abuse are ill-equipped to develop the social competence they will need to advance to sexual skills.

Those boys whose fathers are absent tend to avoid situations such as father/son events that might provide them with the appropriate tools for success in relationships. And fully fifty percent of fathers are absent, either through death, abandonment, divorce, or imprisonment. Still others may be present physically, but not emotionally. With no role model and no one to turn to, these boys are unable to form close attachments to other men and grow up lonely and isolated.

More often than not, other events occur that reinforce the sense of isolation. A move to a distant city, the loss of a pet, money problems, breakup of a relationship—things that normal people can cope with—in such cases could be the final defeat that sends the pre-criminal over the edge into serial murder. Half of the killers Ressler interviewed admitted that they had never had a consenting sexual experience with another adult—and they resented it. In the case of homosexual killers, there tends to be a preference for bondage, torture and sado-masochism in their short-term relationships.

In order to carry out their monstrous acts, the killer must depersonalize the victim and make them into an object that is less than human. Victims are chosen who are weaker than the perpetrator, victims who cannot effectively fight back.

Formula for the deviant personality:

- *Distant mother*
- *Absent or abusive father (and abusive siblings)*
- *Disinterested school system*
- *Ineffective social services system*
- *Inability to relate sexually in a normal manner*

This formula produces includes the following childhood behaviors:

✓ *Inability to give or receive affection*
✓ *Self-destructive behavior*
✓ *Cruelty to pets*
✓ *Stealing*
✓ *Lack of self-control*
✓ *Lack of long-term friends*
✓ *Unable to make eye contact*
✓ *Preoccupation with fire, blood and gore*
✓ *Learning disorders*
✓ *Lying*

But when it suits their needs of the moment, the more manipulative type of sociopath is able to appear attractive, bright, loving, and helpless.

Two types of killers

Ressler identifies two types of serial killers, the organized and the disorganized. Two-thirds are the organized type. Following are some of the characteristics associated with this type:

• *Often has a "normal" appearing relationship and a decent job (Gerald Schaefer, the "Sex Beast" of Florida was a married policeman).*
• *Keeps 'trophies' of his crimes (e.g.: jewelry, items of clothing, or body parts).*
• *Enjoys violent pornography.*
• *Seeks to make his fantasies a reality.*
• *Stalks his victims, who are carefully selected.*
• *Generally kills each victim in a similar manner, using similar weapons (i.e., gun, knife, strangulation, etc.).*
• *Feels entitled to anything he wants (egocentric).*

The Organized Killer

The organized killer often appears attractive and outgoing. Ted Bundy even had the judge in his case expressing regret that he had to sentence Bundy to death. Westley Allen Dodd, who was executed in Washington state in early 1993, was able to lure young boys with the promise of a trip to McDonalds and to K-Mart to buy toys.

In school, this type may have been the class clown or a bully. His behavior made other people notice him. His sense of superiority gives him delusions of grandeur. Although he may have many short-term sexual partners, long-term relationships are unlikely. He may have had a father in the home who worked steadily, but who gave inconsistent discipline.

During an interview on the CNN Special Reports broadcast, *Murder By Number,* Westley Dodd claimed that he came from a "normal" home. "We had a car and a TV and a nice house," he said, "I was never abused." However, when you examine his handwriting (further in this paper) you may draw a different conclusion. One wonders how an abused child knows what abuse is when they have nothing to compare to. They believe that the behavior perpetrated on them is normal and goes on in everyone's home.

The Disorganized Killer

- *May have mental problems.*
- *Probably doesn't drive a car.*
- *Uses whatever weapon may be at hand.*
- *Mutilates the body.*
- *Makes no attempt to hide the evidence or prevent identification.*
- *Picks victims at random.*

The disorganized type of serial killer has a poor self-image. Unlike the organized type, he may be unattractive and even have a physical disability that makes him feel different and uncomfortable. He feels and acts inadequate and is an underachiever, which serves to reinforce his anger and isolation.

Unable to relate to others, he becomes a loner. He doesn't know how to express his emotions properly, which results in internalized hurt, frustration, anger, and fear. At school, he was probably quiet and docile—no one remembers him. At home, alcoholism is a likely component of the family dynamic, with a father whose work was unsteady and who gave harsh discipline. With the disorganized type, mental illness may be present in the family, such as a schizophrenic mother who was unable to properly nurture her child.

The handwriting of the serial killer

Although it would be handy if we could neatly pre-package a syndrome of traits to instantly identify a serial killer, or any other type of criminal, it just can't be done. There is no such thing as a "criminal handwriting."

Certainly, there are red flags that the professional analyst should be aware of, but do not expect to find a "this means that" relationship of a single stroke or letter to a personality trait or personality type.

A handwriting sample must always be examined as a whole, and even when identifying numerous negative characteristics, it cannot simply be assumed that the writer will act out their impulses. Having said that, it is important to note that there may be only one tiny indicator in the bigger picture that will be repeated in the writing, that gives a *clue* to the criminal personality, but it is not conclusive.

Thanks to their ability to separate their criminal personality from the one they use in everyday life the psychopath is often able to fool lie detector tests and truth serums. Unfortunately, in many cases, the same seems to hold true for the handwriting samples that are available for study. If the killer doesn't feel guilty about his acts, the clues in the handwriting will be harder, and sometimes not possible, to find.

The handwriting of "run of the mill" criminals is often copybook school-style, which serves as a persona to cover over the true personality. In general, the strongly copybook writer is someone who is a follower with little originality, and when they follow the wrong crowd or idea, tragedy and mayhem often result. This is more apt to be the case with disorganized serial killers than organized ones, who often have more than average intelligence (such as Bundy).

Handwriting while in long-term custody

An important note about the following samples is that most of them were written during the killer's incarceration. Samples penned during the time immediately surrounding the killings tend to have differences. The spatial picture, slant, and other features change significantly and show the loosening of controls. The ductus (line of ink) becomes muddy, dirty-looking, the writing may look agitated.

Westley Dodd kept a diary during the time he was killing young boys, which revealed wider spacing, sharp points in the lower zone, with heavy pools of ink clogging the ductus. The slant leaned further rightward.

While he was imprisoned, Dodd's writing becomes much more compact, rigid, and upright because he was forced to follow a strict set of rules and regulations. He was unable to act on his murderous fantasies.

During the videotaped interviews with serial killers Jeffrey Dahmer, Westley Dodd, Christine Falling, and others, they all displayed what psychologists refer to as a flat affect. Their faces were expressionless and they referred to the murders as if they had happened to someone else ("the thing that happened"). The one exception was Westley Dodd, who seemed to have some remorse, but even he admitted that it was not sufficient to keep him from killing again.

One important common thread in many of the serial killer samples is the rigidity, the lack of emotional release, and a distorted personal pronoun (capital I). However, no handwriting analyst would be able to look at these samples, not knowing who they were, and be able to say unequivocally, "That's a serial killer!" These samples don't look so different from the writings of people we meet every day.

It is important, though, to remember: if you see one small unusual characteristic that is repeated, even a few times, in the writing, don't ignore it. It might be the only item that looks "odd," in which case, it deserves extra attention. *Still, such a characteristic must always be interpreted within the context of the whole writing sample.*

For example, the t-crossings in Robert Long's sample are extremely long and heavy. The fact is, most people who make long t crossings are not serial murderers. The key in Long's case is, the t-crossings *in the whole picture of his writing, which reveals extreme rigidity,* should be viewed as a red flag.

Without that degree of rigidity, extremely long t-crossings in a handwriting sample from an applicant for a sales or marketing job might add to his ability to do the job. But in combination with the type of rigidity we see in Long's sample, we would know that this is a very controlling, aggressive person who would be a "retention risk" (a euphemism for "you may want to pass on the opportunity to hire this person.")

Another example is seen in the handwriting of Carol Bundy (no relation to Ted), which looks just like any number of "normal" writings, with one small exception. Some of the oval letters are filled with pools of ink. This is something that might be overlooked if the analyst didn't realize they were dealing with a sociopath.

To illustrate the *limitations* of handwriting analysis, included in this paper is a sample of a kind-hearted person who would never hurt anyone, yet whose handwriting could be construed as someone with the potential for violence.

The key word here is *potential.* Handwriting demonstrates potential but cannot with certainty forecast behavior.

The writer of this sample grew up in a home dominated by a smothering mother who did not provide positive nurturing. Discipline was harsh and this man was continually castigated and demeaned for anything he tried to do. Yet, he was tied to his mother and has always lived only a few miles away from his childhood home. His father was present but emotionally beaten down and ineffectual in the face of the mother's controlling behavior.

In the end, abused children grow up to be fine, honorable citizens, some develop multiple personalities, some become killers, and all the variations along the spectrum. As in all areas of life, a wide array of factors comes into play, including genetics, environment, and temperament blending together to determine the outcome.

The next section presents a series of handwriting samples written by convicted serial killers and a brief analysis of each.

Westley Allen Dodd

Convicted of the murder of three young boys, Dodd requested to be executed by hanging, stating that he knew that if he were to be released he would continue killing. To him, murder became a thrilling obsession that claimed his every waking moment.

In an interview for the CNN Special Report, *Murder By Number,* Dodd outlined how he first killed two young brothers by stabbing and strangulation. He was somehow grotesquely touched when, after he had stabbed the first boy to death and was running after the second, who had momentarily escaped, the child looked up at him and said "I'm sorry." Unfortunately, it did not save the boy's life.

It was only a short time after that Dodd pursued his third victim, a four-year-old. He described how he lured the child away from his older brother where they were playing in the park, with promises of hamburgers at McDonalds and toys from K Mart. He took the boy to his apartment, sexually assaulted him and during the night whispered, "I'm going to kill you."

After taking this little boy's life, Dodd went to work, thinking obsessively all day about what he was going to do to the body, which he had hung in his closet like a slab of beef, even though rigor mortis had set in.

He was caught in Washington state at a movie theater, attempting to abduct an older boy from the men's room there. As he pulled the boy from the theater, the boy was crying out for help, "He's killing me," not knowing how close to the truth he was. Nonetheless, Dodd managed to get the boy into his car. Fortunately, he was having car trouble and it was for this reason that he was unable to escape capture.

Westley Dodd blamed the system for his behavior, stating that he felt he could do whatever he wanted to. He was actually only prosecuted for a small number of the crimes he committed. Dodd's handwriting in the sample above was taken from the diary he kept while on his murderous spree. Compare it to the one on the next page, which was written after some time in prison.

The prison sample below is remarkable due to two important features—the spatial arrangement. The extremely close spacing indicates that he was emotionally needy (again, close spacing), but didn't know when to stop and didn't have any idea of the appropriate means to get his needs met. He suffered from a complete lack of boundaries. In addition, the rigidity shows the lack of release that built up until the next kill.

Dodd could prey on only children because they were weaker than he and he could force them to submit to him. The "flame shaped" loops—upper loops with a twist at the tops—indicate twisted thought patterns and point to a possible head injury.

The rigidity of the writing (lack of balance between contraction and release in the writing rhythm) shows his need to be in control at all times. This results from a fear that if he allowed others to control him, he would go completely wild—which of course he did anyway when he murdered. The pressure pattern appears to be variable, with light and dark patches all through the sample. This demonstrates his inconsistent feelings and behavior and inability to control himself and is often a factor in the handwritings of criminals.

Arthur Shawcross

The subject of a book titled *Misbegotten Son,* Arthur Shawcross lived and killed in the Rochester, New York area. He was convicted of murdering eleven prostitutes, but that was after he had served fourteen years for the rape and murder of an eight-year-old girl. Even though he also admitted killing a young boy, he was able to plea bargain his way out of a conviction. His defense consisted of a complicated combination of the insanity pleas, PTSD (he served in Vietnam), and a claim of multiple personality caused by abuse as a child. Robert Ressler was quickly able to shoot down the PTSD claims, while another doctor managed to disprove the others. Shawcross received ten consecutive life sentences. He died in prison in 2008 due to cardiac arrest.

The following samples of Shawcross's writing, like Westley Dodd's, have nothing special to distinguish them from the average person's. However, his printing has some aberrations. For instance, some letters seem to unexpectedly fall over to the right, suggesting sudden, explosive behavior. The middle zone varies in size, and the slant is mixed, again showing inconsistency and impulsiveness in feelings and behavior.

> ? psychosis could be explained in terms
> [o]f Freudian or Jungian theroy. But was
> [i]t possible that some people were rotton
> [f]rom the start, hopelessly corrupt before
> [e]nvironment had an opportunity to effect

The wide spacing between the words reveal his isolation and lack of connection to others. Many words slant down, an indicator of depression. Some letters bounce off the baseline, suggesting abrupt moments of elation.

> No interview at this time but I am giving you a letter to the world at large. Something someone should really think about.

His cursive writing above is undeveloped copybook style. There is no originality. The upper zone is too tall. He likes to make rules for others but not follow them himself. Not the stunted lower zone, which shows a lack of appropriate sexual release.

Jeffrey Dahmer

One of the most infamous serial killers, Jeffrey Dahmer was captured in 1991, after killing, mutilating, and cannibalizing at least 17 victims. He began killing in 1978 at the age of 18 when he picked up a hitchhiker and murdered him, without a plan and without a motive. It was another nine years before he killed again.

From 1987 in the Wisconsin area, his grisly activities escalated as he lost his sense of caution and began to experience feelings of omnipotence—he believed he could not be caught. And even though he had left evidence in plain sight in his apartment for months prior to his arrest, police, his landlord, and others who visited failed to note anything unusual.

A necrophiliac, Dahmer not only committed post-mortem sex acts on his victims, he ate their flesh and retained some of their body parts, seeing these souvenirs as a way to keep them close to him. When interviewed by Robert Ressler, Jeffrey Dahmer was unable to relate to the crimes with which he was charged. He simply could not understand how he had done these things.

His impoverished printed writing, done prior to his arrest and trial for murder and cannibalism, is devoid of any loops (loops are manifest containers for emotions). He could not relate to his crimes because he has no connection to humanity.

My name is Jeff Dahmer. On Sept. 20/78 I was arrested in Milwaukee WI. for taking pictures of a 13 yr. old miner. On Sept. 27, 1988 I was released on bail from the Mil. Co. jail. On May 24, 1989 after having entered a plea of guilty in your court I received my sentence. It was as follows, One year on work release at CCC, and five years of probation. I have, as of this date, served six months and four days of my sentence. Sir, I have always believed that o

Although there are some wide spaces between words, line spacing is too crowded. However, since Dahmer was writing from prison, we don't know whether is access to writing material were limited, forcing him to write closer than he otherwise might.

The left tending lower zone is seeking an identity, looking for the nurturing that Jeffrey must have lacked. A striking feature of this writing is the holes along the ductus (writing line). Especially in oval letters, the bottom is open, signifying his lack of morality. This particular characteristic only appears in extremely dangerous criminals, usually rapists and murderers.

His later writing after a long period of incarceration reveals the unsatisfied needs and urges in the extreme lower lone length, which interferes with the lines below. In the absence of an outlet, the frustration was building. Dahmer was brutally murdered by another convict while serving his sentence.

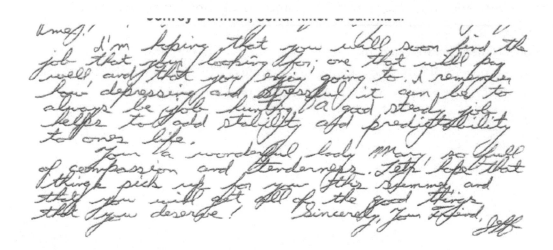

Christine Falling

Although most serial killers are men, a Florida babysitter, Christine Falling claimed her place in this bizarre clique. Christine's 16-year old mother was a prostitute who chose not to keep her children. Christine claims that her foster parents were abusive and that at the age of six, she witnessed the father sexually assaulting her younger sister. In the videotaped interview of CNN, she recounts how she tried to call for help on the kitchen phone, but all of a sudden felt the cord wrapped around her neck by her foster father. The two girls were placed in a children's home by police for a year.

At age 14 Christine married a man in his twenties. After six weeks that included violent battles, they separated and she began claiming various illnesses that took her to the hospital 54 times in one year. It was during this period that Christine contacted her biological mother, asking to live with her.

However, when the girl refused to allow her mother to make a prostitute of her, her mother hit her in the head with a wooden board, resulting in hospitalization. Christine subsequently began having grand mal seizures.

Obese and unattractive, Christine had difficulty getting work. She began babysitting for friends and relatives, caring for hundreds of children. It was actually her infant niece who became her first victim. Christine was sitting in the car with the child, while the mother went into a store. She says she doesn't know how, but her hands simply found their way around the baby's neck and she was dead.

Thus, began a chain of killings—at least six. Finally, after someone noticed that several infants had died in her care and under questioning, she admitted to killing the children. She claimed "voices" had told her to do it. In 1982 Christine Falling was given a life sentence with eligibility for parole in 2007. She wants to go back to babysitting. "I just love kids to death," she said. Her request for parole was denied.

Hello! How are you
doing? Fine I hope. Me
well pretty good I suppose. I
was just thinking about you so
I thought I would sit down
and write you a letter. I really
enjoyed the interview with you.
And anytime you want to do
another with me just be sure
to let me know and I will
be more than happy to do one.
I wanted to thank you very
much for the photos and
everything. I also wanted to ask

It may be that the twisted upper zone is a reflection of the head trauma Christine suffered. Certainly, her thinking is distorted. The large, rounded writing with middle zone emphasis looks like that of a young girl, yet Christine is in her thirties. She is emotionally immature, seeing herself as the center of the universe. This, in effect, gives her permission to take what she wants, including the lives of children. She is so completely subjective that it doesn't occur to her that someone else's needs might take precedence.

Several letters form an 'x' below the baseline, which some analysts interpret as self-destructive behavior. The extremely low t-crossings show her lack of ambition or energy to change. Wide spacing suggests the lack of close alliances and a sense of detachment from her fellow man.

This oral writing signifies someone whose most basic human needs were neglected at the earliest stage of life. As a result, Christine is constantly seeking what she missed, but the void in her life, symbolized by the large circular letters, can never be filled.

Richard Ramirez

Richard Ramirez, known as the Night Stalker, terrorized Southern California in 1985, torturing, raping, and killing numerous victims. He was a self-professed devil worshiper. He was finally caught and nearly killed by a mob when he was attempting to steal a car.

This sample was written after many years in prison. The simplified forms reveal his intelligence. The red flag areas are the extremes in the lengths, which create zonal imbalance and show avoidance of middle zone reality. The lower zone thins out, which is often seen in impotent males. The extreme wide word spaces are a sign of his emotional isolation.

Of all the samples in this paper, Ramirez' looks least like one that might be attributed to a heinous killer and yet the level of evil in his acts is virtually unfathomable. There are few signs of stress that might be created by guilt or remorse. Ramirez died of complications from lymphoma while in prison.

Robert Joseph Long

Bobby Joe Long had a history of head trauma beginning with a serious head injury at the age of five when he fell off a swing and impaled his eyelid with a stick. The next year he was thrown from his bike and crashed head-first into a parked car. This accident resulted in the loss of several teeth and a severe concussion. At age seven he fell onto his head from a pony and was left feeling severely dizzy and nauseated for weeks afterwards.

In addition, Bobby Joe suffered from a genetic disorder—an extra X chromosome. This caused him to grow breasts, a humiliating experience for a young boy. At twelve years the extra tissue was surgically removed, but he was left with some gender confusion which was exacerbated by his mother sharing a bed with him. He claims she had him watch while she carried on liaisons with different men, a charge which his mother denies.

While in the army, Bobby Joe crashed a motorcycle, shattering his helmet as it impacted on the street. During his hospitalization he began having violent headaches, alternating with murderous rages and an obsession with sexual activity. Intercourse twice a day with his wife was not enough and he found some release in masturbating five times a day. However, he needed more, and began a reign of terror in Florida from 190 to 1983, as he raped 50 women.

Although he was apprehended Long somehow managed to escape conviction and was soon on a new rampage that escalated to murder. Over a six-month period, he strangled, stabbed and shot 9 victims who he viewed as expendable because they were prostitutes or what he termed "tramps."

His downfall came when he selected a 17-year-old girl as his next prey. She was riding a bicycle home after working late at a donut shop, when he reached out from his parked van and grabbed her. Her thirty-six-hour ordeal ended only after he had blindfolded and repeatedly raped her. She kept begging him to spare her life, telling him he could do what he wanted, if only he would let her go. The teenager was able to see around the corner of the blindfold, enough to identify the make and model of Long's car and a bank where he used an ATM.

Shortly after his stop at the bank, he ordered her out of the car. She feared for her life, but he told her to stay where she was and not move for five minutes. When she looked, he was gone.

Why did Bobby Joe Long not kill this girl? Was it because he felt sorry for her? According to the CNN program, it was because something just didn't "fit." She was not like the others. Long remains on death row.

The writing looks angry and rigid. The *potential* for violent acting out is seen in the slashing t-bars and i dots in combination with the angles, heavy pastosity, and abrupt endings.

The printing, with its extra-long but incomplete lower zones, reveal his intense frustration. Again, we see the isolation, demonstrated by the very wide spacing, in this case, between the letters. The sample was reduced for space.

I hate to even waste the time, stamp, and ink to write this, but I wanted to tell you what a punk you are.

Several people have told me what a sensationalized, negative piece you did, using my name and situation.

My mistake ... I actually thought CNN was a cut above that ... but I see it's not.

Carol Bundy

Carol Bundy worked as a nurse before her conviction for murdering her lover. She died in prison of heart failure after serving more than twenty years. She and another boyfriend, Doug Clark, were convicted of several murders of young prostitutes. In one case, Bundy claimed that Clark masturbated into the severed head of a young victim.

Like Christine Falling's her handwriting is round and flabby-looking. There is no "backbone." The spatial arrangement is weak and letters that are filled in with ink are the red flag in this case, suggesting a "damming up" of base desires, which exploded into her murderous activities.

but I am better off in here simply because I have no way of making a living and no way of taking care of myself. The issue is probably moot for me anyway as I don't think I'll live too much longer, no more than a few more years. Certainly I'll be dead before I'm 50, and it may be sooner than that.

Well, Teresa, I'll close now. Thanks again for the favor, and the interest.

Best,
Carol Bundy

Ted Bundy

Ted Bundy was executed in 1989, a sadistic rapist who killed at least 30 women and possibly many more. He preyed on attractive young women by pretending to be injured, then he would assault and kidnap them, performing sex acts on their corpses after he had killed them.

Bundy was raised to believe that his mother was his sister. He was said to be close to his grandparents. However, other family members described his grandfather as a tyrant and a bully. The movement patterns in his handwriting are profoundly disturbed, indicating issues with his ego and a battered self-esteem. The extremely long, initial strokes are like a harpoon that literally hook in his victims. The presence of those harpoon-like lead-in strokes is a major red flag. They are especially easy to see at the beginnings of lines. They signify the extreme hostility that is hidden below the baseline (in the subconscious). The hooks hold on to the past and any real or imagined hurts.

The rhythm is slack, lazy, and the weak hooks in some of the lower zone forms suggest impotence. Other lower zone forms are wide loops that pull to the left, which is often seen in writers who never felt loved. The leftward trend is constantly moving back to the past, seeking the mothering and nurturing they felt they lacked. In other samples, the personal pronoun I (not present in this one) is overly-inflated on the top, demonstrating an unrealistic view of women.

Additionally, the spacing is weak (crowded), a feature we see over and over in these serial murderers who feel the desire to control all space.

Cary Stayner

Cary Stayner's story is extraordinarily tragic. His younger brother Stephen was kidnapped and held captive for more than seven years before escaping. All the while, as one can imagine, their parents grieved their lost son, while the one who was still at home felt overlooked and neglected. Compounding the tragedy, nine years after Stephen escaped and returned home, he was killed in a motorcycle accident. His life was the subject of a 1989 Emmy-nominated mini-series, *I Know My First Name Is Steven.*

Cary Stayner claims he was molested by an uncle when he was eleven. He unsuccessfully attempted suicide at age 30. While working as a handyman at a motel close to Yosemite National Park 1999, he murdered two women and two teenagers there, decapitating one of them. Cary had no previous record and was calm when he was interviewed about the murders, so at first was not considered a suspect in the killings. Later, when arrested, he claimed to have fantasized about murdering women even before the abduction of his brother. He pled not guilty by reason of insanity but was found sane and convicted. He is on death row at San Quentin.

His handwriting contains a major red flag: the disproportionally tall upper zone, which, especially when the loops are narrow, is a strong indicator for the authoritarian personality. This in itself does not reveal him to be a killer, but the extremely tall upper zone is often seen in men (rare in women) who have a profound need to be in control because inside they feel so weak.

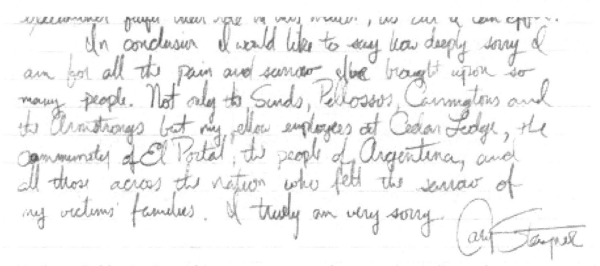

Similar to Bobby Joe Long, his t-crosses are too long, another indicator for strong control needs. The lower zone is stunted, indicating sexual frustration.

Other than these indicators, his handwriting looks fairly average. This is one more reason why it is important to be aware of the red flags in handwriting and pay attention to them. They might not tell you that the writer is a serial killer, but they are a marker for pathological behavior.

Aileen Wuornos

A Florida prostitute, Aileen Wuornos was convicted of killing seven of her customers. She was executed in 2002. Wuornos was born to a 15-year-old girl and a father who was in prison for the rape and attempted murder of a child. She was abandoned by her mother and raised by her alcoholic, abusive grandparents.

By the time she was 14, Aileen was pregnant after being raped by a friend of her grandfather. At 15 she was living in the woods and supporting herself as a prostitute. Her life seemed to become a series of arrests on a variety of charges.

Her handwriting has the same extremely rigid structure that we have seen in that of other serial killers. The writing hugs the baseline, which represents the need for security (the "ground we stand on.") The writing is conventional copybook, not unintelligent. The word spacing is overall too crowded, indicating her lack of appropriate boundaries. Yet, after punctuation, there are extremely wide spaces. One interpretation might be that she was able to compartmentalize.

Aileen Wuornos was executed in 2002.

Jack the Ripper

Although many letters were received by the police and newspapers, claiming to be the infamous killer, the following sample taken from one of the "Dear Boss" letters, was generally accepted as authentic.

We see little to identify the handwriting below as a "criminal" writing. The spatial arrangement includes wide word space and wide letter spacing and there is a changing pressure pattern that may be interpreted as a red flag. Heavy blotches of ink in other parts of the letter reveal sudden explosions of emotion. There are color copies on Google Images that show the letter written in red ink.

Not a Serial Killer

The last sample, mentioned earlier, was not written by a serial killer, nor any type of criminal. It is included here to demonstrate how an ordinary, decent person's handwriting can include negative influences. Any handwriting analyst might be excused for mistaking the writer of this sample for criminal.

However, while this writer has plenty of emotional issues to deal with and tremendous pent-up anger, he has never behaved violently. The sample was written when he was in his mid-30's. He is now in his mid-70s. Close to being a hoarder, he has a hard time letting go of anything or anyone. He spends a great deal of time and energy helping friends, but if they do not show the appreciation he believes he deserves, he becomes resentful, though rarely expressing those feelings.

Handwriting analysts must never forget their limitations in the heady sense of power that comes with the ability to evaluate personality from a page of handwriting. It is vital that we not judge others, but only describe the behavior that we see in their writing. And always, we must remember that behind every handwriting there is a human being with their own story.

References

Murder by Number, CNN Special Reports, Atlanta, 1993

Magid, Kenneth, PhD, High Risk, Children Without A Conscience, Bantam Books, New York, 1988

Marcuse, Irene, PhD, Guide to the Disturbed Personality Through Handwriting, Arco Publishing Company, New York, 1969

Newton, Michael, Hunting Humans, the Encyclopedia of Serial Killers Volume 1, Avon Books, New York, 1990

Ressler, Robert H. & Tom Shachtman; Whoever Fights Monsters, St. Martin's Paperbacks, New York, 1992

Last Words...

I hope you have found this group of monographs helpful in your continuing studies of handwriting analysis.

In Volume II, with contributions by the late Israeli psychologist Dr. Ze'ev Bar-av, anxiety disorders and personality disorders are examined in how they may be detected in handwriting. The following topics are covered:

- ✓ *Fear, Stress, Anxiety*
- ✓ *Introduction to Adjustment Disorders*
- ✓ *Introduction to Personality Disorders*
- ✓ *Antisocial Personality Disorder*
- ✓ *Borderline Personality Disorder and Histrionic Personality Disorder*
- ✓ *Narcissistic Personality Disorder and Dependent Personality Disorder*
- ✓ *Obsessive-Compulsive Personality Disorder and Paranoid Personality Disorder*
- ✓ *Schizoid Personality Disorder, Schizotypal Personality Disorder, Schizophrenia, Dissociative Identity Disorder*
- ✓ *Why does the graphologist need to know about psychology?*
- ✓ *Freudian Terminology and Handwriting Analysis—do they mesh?*
- ✓ *Anger, Hatred, Hostility, Aggression and Violence, their expression in handwriting*
- ✓ *Reporting Your Results and Sanity-Competency*

About the Author

Sheila Lowe began her study of handwriting in 1967 as a senior in high school. After ten years of reading as many books as she could find, she discovered the Handwriting Analysis Workshop Unlimited courses offered by internationally recognized handwriting expert, Charlie Cole.

Sheila joined the American Handwriting Analysis Foundation, a nonprofit educational organization, and passed their certification examination in 1981. She served on the board of directors as newsletter editor for eight years, and as a chapter president. In 2012, she was elected president of the organization and as of this printing continues in that position, as well as editor of *The Vanguard*.

Sheila is also a Certified Forensic Document Examiner who has been court-qualified since 1985. She currently serves as Ethics Chair for the Scientific Association of Forensic Examiners. Having been appointed to the Judge's Panel of Experts for Los Angeles County, she is retained by various offices of the Public Defender and District Attorneys, and continues to work with private clients and attorneys.

As a frequent speaker for professional and civic groups in the US, Canada and her home country, Great Britain, Sheila teaches on many handwriting topics. She has appeared many times in the media when there are questions about handwriting.

Sheila has authored several books and monographs about handwriting analysis. Her Handwriting Analyzer software has been in use worldwide since 1997. She offers a self-paced online study program in Gestalt Graphology. Her award-winning Forensic Handwriting Mystery series featuring fictional handwriting expert Claudia Rose and her partner, LAPD Detective Joel Jovanic.

Sheila lives in Ventura, California.

Made in the USA
Monee, IL
24 May 2020

31767085R00118